More Prepared to Answer

Telling the Greatest Story Ever Told

Mark A. Paustian

Northwestern Publishing House
Milwaukee, Wisconsin

Fourth printing, 2009
Third printing, 2006
Second printing, 2005

Library of Congress Control Number: 2004101856
Northwestern Publishing House
1250 N. 113th St., Milwaukee, WI 53226-3284
© 2004 by Northwestern Publishing House
www.nph.net
Published 2004
Printed in the United States of America
ISBN 978-0-8100-1648-4

CONTENTS

Stories of the Last Days of Christ

Story of the Lord's Resurrection

Story of Pentecost

Conclusion

INTRODUCTION

"Come and see"

Philip had been breathless with excitement. "We have found the one the prophets wrote about, Jesus of Nazareth." The bluntness of Nathanael was only natural. Nathanael was not merely skeptical. He was plainly insulting.

"Nazareth! Can anything good come from there?"

Everyone knew that Judea, not Galilee, was the home of Jerusalem and the seat of all serious Jewishness. Nathanael considered Philip's "Messiah" only marginally Jewish, if Jewish at all. Nevertheless, Philip flashed a knowing smile and a winsome, "Come and see!"

When Jesus and Nathanael finally met, Jesus was disarmingly gracious. His first words to Nathanael were a compliment that suspiciously mirrored Nathanael's contempt. *"Here is a true Israelite,* in whom there is nothing false." Jesus added cryptically, "I saw you while you were still under the fig tree."

Hmmmm. The fig tree was the symbol of Israel as well as the customary shade for Hebrew prayer. And whatever else a "true Israelite" might have been, a true Israelite was someone who was waiting expectantly for the Christ, the long-promised Messiah. "Nathanael, I saw you there. I heard a child of Abraham praying. I know the things you ask for when it's just you and Adonai. Ah, Nathanael." Do you see?

Clearly something more was happening in John chapter 1 than is first apparent. For Nathanael suddenly went all the way in his confession, skipping right past "great teacher" and not pausing at "powerful prophet." His faith just exploded:

"You are the Son of God; you are the King of Israel."

"Because I saw you by a fig tree? You shall see greater things than that," Jesus pledged. The very best things: a flawless life, Compassion and Truth walking around, a spilling of wonders, a blurting out of heaven's best secrets.

Then a brave self-sacrifice.

Then a resurrection.

He would see, to borrow Jesus' picture, a divine and human ladder fusing earth and heaven. And so Nathanael would see who *he* was . . . and what *life* is . . . and who *God* is. As C. S. Lewis commented, "I believe in Christianity as I believe the sun has risen, not only because I see it, but because by it I see everything else."

(Please read John 1:43-51.)

"Come and see," is all Philip said in answer to an ungentle skeptic.

There is, of course, a perfectly good solution to Nathanael's problem with the Messiah who came from Nazareth. Jesus was actually born in the very Judean town that had been prophesied for the Messiah, but his parents fled for their lives from Bethlehem when he was very young. Even if Philip doesn't know all that and is stumped by a rather simple challenge, his confidence in Christ is not misplaced. He is right about Jesus, even if he cannot fully explain why. He knows what he knows, for reasons that resist analysis and defy debate.

This story's message, or one of them, is that we Christians can stay calm in the face of intellectual challenges to our faith. Christian apologist Paul Little loved to say, "After two thousand years, no question is going to bring Christianity crashing." Believer, do you endure the condescension of your philosophy professor? Did you fumble for words when he made you stand up before the class? Did the credibility of Christian truth seem to hinge on a quick reply? Relax. It didn't.

You're still right about Jesus. Your faith will be vindicated in the end, and the world's rebuke will be put to shame. That you believed in Christ crucified and held on when it no longer seemed reasonable, this will be your glory.

> "For the foolishness of God is wiser than man's wisdom, and the weakness of God is stronger than man's strength."[1]

In fact, I cheerfully share syndicated columnist William F. Buckley's admission that the Christian faith is bigger, worlds bigger, than my own powers of description or rational defense. It may sound like a cop-out. But there it is. I know what I know. For two millennia some of the most ingenious of our species, including some of the most evil, have labored hard and long to slam the door on Christianity. As Buckley observed, something is keeping it ajar. Better, *Someone.*

As long as there is God and as long as there is a world, there will always be here and there in that world a sanctuary. "I will build my church,"[2] said the Carpenter, the Christ. There will always be a remnant at peace, with ears sensitive to the sound of his unwavering voice. There will always be those souls made small enough in repentance and intellectual humility to find the narrow door that leads to eternal life. God has seen to it. He loves us all with an eternal, steady, and changeless love.

It is his greatest pleasure to reveal his Son within the likes of one of us.

What you're holding in your hands is a book of rather simple treatments of the questions people often ask of Christians. I don't pretend to exhaust the dialogue I take up with science, with already tiring postmodernism, with philosophy, or with conventional humanistic wisdom. You'll find a scanty two thousand words or less spent on such challenges as inspire many books. I answer skepticism unapologetically with psychological necessities (forgiveness for one, hope for another). I answer with the very simplest of philosophical tenets on which clarity of thought has long depended (our own existence for one and objective truth for another). Most of all, I answer with the historic certainties in, with, and under humanity's greatest movement (the incarnation, the atonement, the resurrection of Jesus Christ). God's Word, the Holy Bible, is my authority, my real reason, and that old Book requires surprisingly few words to end any human debate.

In the beginning, God . . .

All have sinned and fall short . . .

The Word became flesh and dwelt among us . . .

For God so loved the world . . .

In my Father's house are many rooms . . .

You say, "But what about *this?* . . . Have you ever thought of *that?* . . . Can any good thing come *from faith?*" And all I really mean to say is, "Come and see."

For as I pick up the task of writing another book in answer to Christianity's skeptics, I'm aware that God himself doesn't venture to answer every challenge. Just think how easily he could. He could utterly overwhelm the need for faith with arguments and proofs that would leave us not only convinced but also hiding behind trees and rocks. That isn't his way.

He doesn't prove, doesn't argue, doesn't normally drop supernatural hints at our command or whisper into our ears. He doesn't chase away all the mystery. We are sometimes confused, sometimes hurting, sometimes in the dark, with no human prop on which to rest our faith. Still we follow. And his heart swells.

"Jesus, full of joy through the Holy Spirit, said, 'I praise you, Father, Lord of heaven and earth, because you have hidden these things from the wise and learned, and revealed them to little children. Yes, Father, for this was your good pleasure.' "[3]

This is his way. He takes pleasure—profound, bursting delight—in our faith.

He doesn't submit higher evidence of his reality or of his love than those three decades of sheer epiphany that were the life of Christ . . . as if there could be any higher testimony than the "Word made flesh." Since nothing exists that is greater than God himself, he cannot provide a better reason to believe that it is all true than simply to tell us in his own words that it is, in words that "are spirit and they are life."[4]

He answers grim doubt with winsome grace, with the declaration "this one is mine" heard beneath the sound of sprinkling water in Baptism, with the promise "I have so loved you" tasted in the sacramental bread and wine. And our agnosticism shows itself empty in the light of that divine smile. *"Come and see."*

Every Sunday for the better part of a year, 30 or so of us would meet before worship to study the very stories that I'll be sharing with you in the pages ahead.

Having studied the dying question of John the Baptist or Jesus' parable about weeds growing up with wheat or the story of Mary pouring oil out on Jesus' head and feet, we would save time at the end of each class for a single, vital question: Who needs to know this story? That is, what are the questions people are asking for which this story is the right reply?

"Well . . . they think life has no meaning. . . . They accuse the church of hypocrisy. . . . They say all we care about is money."

And then, in the final five minutes of Bible study, we would sometimes even attempt to roleplay the story-telling. We would turn two chairs toward each other in the front of the sanctuary. One person would articulate the skeptical challenge, and the other, after acknowledging the question and probing a little deeper with other thoughtful questions, would begin:

"I wonder if you know about the time Jesus . . . No? . . . May I tell you?"

And as the weeks went by, the experiences drifted back to the class of how people had done this very thing in real life. They had responded to a question or challenge or need with a "Jesus story." Among the class were lifelong Christians delighting in the sudden aware-ness that they knew what to say and had known for a long time.

As for me, I'll never forget the day it was my turn to roleplay. Here's the situation: The woman across from me was pretending to be burdened beneath a shameless past—she wasn't—as if she had trouble believing forgive-ness could be true for her—she didn't. "Have you ever heard about the time a woman was caught in the act of adultery," I began, "and all her bloodthirsty accusers dragged her to Jesus?" And I proceeded to tell the story from John chapter 8.

I relished the details, pausing as Christ bent to scratch the dirt. . . . "Let the one without sin throw the first stone."
. . . And I let the rocks hit the trampled ground. . . . I let

the town square empty out and the reproachful crowd dis-
perse . . . until the woman, so ashamed, looked up into the
face of her Judge, the Man from Galilee.

"Neither do I condemn you," I said into her wide-
opened eyes.

And my roleplay partner, dear woman, very nearly
fell apart.

She wasn't acting anymore, nor was I pretending to witness. We were experiencing the presence of Christ and
the dynamic power of him, the dissolving of every question in that Living Water, that enduring Word.

"Neither do I condemn you!"

A word about this book . . .

This is my second volume expressing a philosophy of personal witnessing that could be called All I Really Need to Know I Learned in Sunday School. My answers to skeptical questions center on the authoritative stories of Christ, which are divinely inspired and embedded so lovely and deeply in the Christian consciousness. This narrative springs from days of Old Testament waiting, meanders through the life and times of Christ, and empties into this New Testament age.

Why answer questions about science or history, philosophy or morality with stories about Jesus? Let those who will not embrace Christianity know not merely *what* but *who* it is that they're denying and what the cost is to them and to him. On the other hand, some objections people have to the faith are quite reasonable, considering everything they've ever heard and everything they have not. So shove back the innocent ignorance about Christ to offer an alternative to all the propaganda. The compelling scenes of his life, in my view, are ideal conversation pieces between my religion—itself a grand, true story—and the story-hungry culture that surrounds it. After all, if anything can make someone a Christian, it is, just once, really seeing Christ.

And heaven itself stands up to applaud, not when millions find their place in the love of God, but when one does. If my books have played any small part, it would be my great joy to hear from you and know *your* story. I could not take up the writer's task if I didn't know that the Lord, who once spoke through a donkey, could use even me; that the same Jesus who fed five thousand people with a little boy's lunch can bless anything. To be used in such a way, to such an end, seems too much to ask. But nothing has ever stopped God, whose servant I am.

His,
Mark Paustian

"Where was God when I needed him?"

"How long, O Lord? Will you forget me forever?"

So wrote King David from his sickbed, tortured by painful thinking, yet unable to set it aside. "How long will you hide your face from me? How long must I wrestle with my thoughts and every day have sorrow in my heart?"

"Ad-a-NAH!" is the sound of the ancient Hebrew word that David cried out four times.

"How long?" Literally, "Until when?"

It puts a picture into my mind of God pouring into King David's cup as a father would pour milk into a cup for a child, whispering, "Say when." Only, what poured so freely was pain into his mind and disease into his body. David cried, "Enough already! When!" Still God kept pouring, until David was lost in the dreadful feeling of abandonment, in the appalling thought that God had turned his face away.

Scripture says God won't give you more than you can handle, but that threshold seemed long past for David, so he cried out, "Ad-a-NAH, Adonai! Ad-a-NAH? When, Lord, WHEN?"

This is the cry of all humanity. All of humankind lies in the sickbed with King David. What is wrong with everything—all the sin, the shame, the futility, all the fractured relationships, the suffer-

ing children, the rumors of wars, the shadow of death—
when put all together, becomes this one, weary,
anguished cry.

"Until when?"

Such a curious thing, to find in a three-thousand-year-
old hymn my own soul's complaint, the one each of us
thought was private and our own. The God who inspired
these words clearly knows the real me. And he knows
when to say "When."

This time it's a Greek word, *"ho-te,"* and it is found in
Galatians chapter 4.

"When the time had fully come, God sent his Son," who
slipped barely noticed into the warm lake of humanity.
And so, after Mary's labor pains and the anguish of childbirth that went on God knows how long, she was the first
one to look into the gray eyes of this infant and ponder
the imponderable fact.

"It's really you."

(Please read Psalm 13 and Galatians 4:4-6.)

You look back on times in your life when the pain or confusion or sorrow got so bad that you cried out to God with
all your heart, "Where are you?" And he answered?

Nothing. (Or so you thought.)

Our hearts naturally lean away from God as it is, with
resistance deeper than consciousness and stubbornness we
cannot begin to justify. So in times of suffering or gut-
punching disappointment, people can find the temptation
irresistible to declare themselves rid of God and to resolve to
move on without him, this God who does nothing when
they need him most. Where is he?

Although he neglects none of his own promises, God still
fails some test of the people's own devising. People taste

some things in times of shame or anguish that they know they never want to taste again. And they resolve right then and there that it is going to be up to them to make sense of life on their own, to reach for whatever satisfactions are available in this world, to feel what they want to feel, and to survive. Alone. Whatever it takes.

Now I even hear people speak this language—*Where in the world is God?*—when they become pregnant out of wedlock or are fired from another job for irresponsibility: "Lord, how could you?" You don't need me to point out the irony here. Sometimes life is a mess because we are. Then what we need, first of all, is for someone to help us read our own stories properly. We reap what we sow.

And yet we all also suffer in ways that aren't particularly our fault. The first thing I want to tell you if you're asking, "Where was God when I needed him?" is that it's okay to say such things out loud. For the reassurance that this is so, do turn to Psalm 13, which was described earlier. The first time I found that spot in the Bible—the first time its words opened up to me—was when my bride of a couple months fell deathly ill and would scream out in pain. I've been leading people to that holy ground ever since. You might as well bring to God what is really in you, not what you think is *supposed* to be in you, even if your question has a serrated edge: "God, where are you!?"

What we're always needing to get down to, when it comes to a relationship with God, is "the real me talking to the real You." Not me as an actor on a stage talking to a god of my own distorted invention. Let it be *God* as he reveals himself in Holy Scripture and *me* as he is so prone to reveal me in the same place. All of us at some time or another are confronted by our human frailty, by the weakening of our bodies, by the inevitability of our deaths. We face every day the limitations of our spirits. We long to love and to live meaningfully, to connect with people in real relationships, and to soar. So let us cry, not what is supposed to be in us, but what is.

"How long, O Lord?"

I ask you to bring yourself and your tear-stained questions to God. " 'For I know the plans I have for you,' declares the LORD, 'plans to prosper you and not to harm you, plans to give you hope and a future.' "[5] What *are* the plans? We are dying to know. So the verse goes on: " '. . . when you seek me with all your heart. I will be found by you,' declares the LORD."[6] That's the plan. The reality of God is sometimes felt most in his apparent absence. You may seek him in the dark with a passion you could never muster in the daylight.

I understand what makes your heart ask, "Can there really be a God of love?" Yet before you can measure his compassion or his resolve, my task is to suggest another question, "What is our deepest need?" People who answer that the deepest needs of people are to be wealthy or healthy, beautiful or pain free, will always conclude that God must love some people and not others. Say that the needs that matter most have to do with being surrounded by happy things or by nice people and, if your premise is true, it might be fair to question the depth of God's care. However, once you recognize that we all share equally in One Great Need—our need as sinners is to have peace with God—the others are reduced to insignificance, and everything is changed. In other words, look in the mirror.

If you've ever surprised yourself by the bad thing—the selfish or mean or cowardly thing—you were capable of, in that moment, sin's eternal consequences suddenly made terrible sense. Every other difficult thing in the world was trivial, a secondary concern next to the problem of peace with God. And the real truth of the matter was that even before you did that awful thing, your need was just as desperate, just as absolute. Self-righteousness kept you from seeing it.

If you still can't see your gaping spiritual need, then ask, at least, *what if it were true?* What if what is really wrong with everything is human sin? What if, as the Scriptures say, it is God that is the wronged one, the disappointed one? What if all that has gone wrong is humanity's fault, not his, but our minds are so clouded in sin and shrouded in death that we can't see it? What if when we blame God for things we don't understand or rage in senseless atheistic hatred at him for not existing . . . well . . . what if we're wrong? What if nothing less than eternity is at stake, nothing less than where we will be and how it will be for us forever?

Then the last thing we really need from the God who is there—the *very* last thing—are sweet and pleasant lives that never confront us with our own true condition.

On the other hand, if you could only begin to plumb the depth of humanity's need for a simple thing called forgiveness, called mercy, you might ask your question again, this time with appropriate humility: Where was God when I needed him?

He answered with a crucifixion. God, who exists in sublime independence, chose to enter a relationship with us that would cost him everything and us nothing. For our One Great Need, the Father gave his One and Only Son. On the cross, as someone has pointed out, we witness the greatest miracle in the Bible, the miracle of restraint—when the Father sat on his own hands, doing nothing at all. But how!? How could the one who exploded from heaven, "This is my Son whom I love," possibly hold himself back? Because, you see, he also loved *us*. And so came Jesus' time of no miracle, no answer, no help.

I write a mystery: Where was God when God needed him? See him there, nailed to a tree, crying, bleeding, suffering, dying, and not saying "When" until it was enough . . . not arching his back and pushing on the nails and shouting his triumph, "It is finished," until it really was and the whole world, full of people like you, was redeemed.

I honor your questions. It is good that you ask them. I only ask that we move the conversation to this new ground, this raised plot called Golgotha, where the great human complaint loses all its steam . . . if, in fact, this smattering of blood is God's. It may not even be the questions themselves that are changed, only the heart with which you ask them. For there he stands on the other side of your death, alive with healing in his wings. A woman glances up from inconsolable weeping. He says, "Mary . . ." and she is consoled.

If this is true—and, my friend, it is—then there are new thoughts for you to think, and God himself will pour them into your weary mind by his own comforting Spirit—that his love is unfailing, that you can trust him, that your spirit rejoices in God your Savior. These too are the thoughts of Psalm 13. Read it to the end. The "How long, O LORD?" gives way to a new thing, fresh from him.

"I will sing to the LORD, for he has been good to me."[7]

I realize that it seems God has given you more than you can handle, that it seems like far too much for you to take . . . yet here you are. The miracle is that people who have suffered the most are often the ones singing loudest at Christmas, "Peace on earth and mercy mild, God and sinners reconciled." Not because God's peace and mercy are *supposed* to be in them, but because they *are*. Theirs is a heart-pounding intimacy with God, of a kind and a strength never dreamed of by people who have never known pain.

" 'I will be found by you,' declares the LORD."

There is a depth to these people, not *in spite* of the things he has allowed into their lives—he doesn't do it lightly—but *because* of them. God has taught their knees to bend before the holy child of Bethlehem and their mouths to sing those words: "God and sinners reconciled." It's the real me . . . and it's really you.

The disciples were getting beaten by the storm on the Sea of Galilee. The wind rose up and battered them. They rowed till their arms ached, past 3 A.M., getting nowhere. Where was Jesus when they needed him? He was watching and aching, sighing and crying. It is he who left heaven and entered the very center of human distress to pray to his Father *from there*. And, at just the right time, he was on his way.

"It is I. Don't be afraid."[8]

And he's on his way for you. So be strong. Hold on. Endure. "When Christ, who is your life, appears, then you also will appear with him in glory."[9]

My God will know when to say "When."

"How can there be a good God when the world is such a bad place?"

He got old. That young man who leaned on Jesus' chest the night before the cross, the one who bested Peter in the early morning dash to the tomb—the first one to see the empty grave clothes and believe their mute testimony—finally slowed down.

That John got old is not a remarkable fact all by itself. But then consider that he was the only one of the 12 disciples to accomplish it. He endured, with a mix of sadness and swelling joy, the brutal martyrdom of most from that intimate circle of friends. History records how the people would carry John, the last living link to the One and Only, up to the front of their assemblies so he could deliver his sermon in five words.

"Little children, love one another."

The man had the mind of Christ.

And the day arrived when the Breath of Heaven moved John to write it all down and gave John the very words for the gospel that bears his name. And so he wrote his marvelous treatment on the subject of Jesus, his Lord and his Friend, so that we would know and believe that Jesus is the Son of God. The hand moved. The page filled. And this is what it said:

"In him was life, and that life was the light of men. The light shines in the darkness, but the darkness has not understood it."

(Please read John chapter 1.)

"How can there be a good God when the world is such a bad place?"

I appreciate this question. It's born of good instincts. It comes from conscience, that undeniable sense of the way things ought to be. The problem? A God of absolute Power as well as absolute Goodness seems incompatible with a world filled with pain and death.

I begin with a borrowed analogy. What if there were no such thing as light? Imagine if light just plain didn't exist and eyes to see it did not exist either. Would we be forever asking why it's so *dark* around here? I don't think so. We would not be able to *imagine* such things as light and dark. We would not find ourselves missing the brilliant color of a sunset or aching to see the look on a loved one's face. If there were no such thing as light, these things would be utterly inconceivable, thoughts our minds would not know how to think, words without meaning to us. Sure, it would be dark around here.

But would we *know* it's dark?

Now . . . is there really no such thing as God? Please think about it. What does it mean when we lie on our beds thinking of the way the world *ought* to be? It means that we know there is an Ultimate Goodness to which the world does not conform. Our minds want to say that the idea of a good God doesn't fit our experiences in a world where children suffer and loved ones die . . . but our hearts give us away. These things are bad, and we know in our deepest parts that they are. So what we really believe, we are startled to discover, is that there is such a thing as Goodness. There has to be. We know what the word means.

A friend of mine was recently overpowered by the awfulness of the world, so much so that he asked me to lunch just to talk about it. Shaking experiences had come to him in quick succession, from a grisly crash on the highway to a startling image on the evening news that managed to sneak past his defenses. But it is precisely this feeling, finding and knowing ourselves to be in a bad place—the longing, aching, and missing the way things ought to be—that shows us what we really believe. The dark torments us precisely because there is such a thing as Light, and we know it full well.

"How can there be a good God when the world is such a bad place?" Rather than try to answer, I really should be insisting that you justify the question. Does it even make sense? By stating the problem the way you do, you clearly believe that you live in a moral universe, that is, one that is supposed to be one way and not another. Why else would you frame the question in a moral way? You are actually assuming the existence of an ultimate Moral Lawgiver, because that is necessary for Good and Bad to have any objective meaning or independent reality. (Without God, Good and Bad are nothing more than human constructions, thoughts in our own heads, and certainly not valid arguments about anything.) So this persistent protest about the sorry state of the world, in trying to deny God, unconsciously appeals to his Reality. What is really going on? To be separated from God by virtue of our own sin is to be cast into a bewildering darkness so deep that we insist it is all there is. Yet our visceral complaints about the dark are our unwitting homage to the Light.

The really startling thing is finding out, in the middle of our gravest doubts about God, what we actually know to be true. I refer to the natural knowledge of God, around which, it is only fair to warn you, an agnostic can never be too careful. Your observation that this world is home to unspeakably bad things may refute such popular notions as pantheism easily enough—is the god-who-is-everything both evil *and* good? both hatred *and* love?—but it swings you closer to Christianity than you realize. Christianity, this ancient faith, has always painted the portrait of an achingly beautiful, tragically spoiled world in a way that conforms perfectly to reality and to the experience of every human being.

So too is the Bible's explanation for the origin of evil perfectly compatible with the existence of a God whose goodness and power are both infinite. Our culture is committed to the notion that freedom of choice is the highest good and that people must be allowed to make their own moral choices. If there's anything we would be willing to call evil nowadays, it would be someone exercising brute power to negate that freedom. Why does it not follow, then, that evil might have originated when a good God gave a good choice to the first human beings and did not use power to prevent them from actually making it? (And anyway, if you want a question that does *not* logically self-destruct, it is that of Saint Augustine: "If there is no God, why is there *so much good* in the world?")

Clearly it's not enough to show inconsistencies in the question this article addresses. Deal with the logical problem as we might, an existential one still remains, precisely because pain does. It hurts to be here. Sometimes a little. Sometimes a lot. If you can just admit that your rational argument holds a contradiction, there will be so much more for you to say to the new questions that may sneak past your defenses.

Michelle was the friend of a friend. At a dinner party, off in our own small corner, we got to talking about religion. She voiced the objection, "How can there be a God of love when the world is the way it is?" Then followed the litany of sorrows—the things she had seen happen to others, the things she had experienced herself. I let her talk. And when she was all through, a response occurred to me that I hadn't thought of before.

"It must be hard," I said slowly and softly.

"What must be hard?"

"To live in a world like this *and to have no God besides.*"

She got quiet for a moment. Then she simply admitted, "Yes . . . it is."

"May I show you a side of God you haven't seen before?" And with that I began to quietly speak to her about Christ. After all, we had finally come down to the question her heart was really asking. Not "How can there be a good God?" but "Where is he? How do I find him in a place like this? I don't see him anywhere." I answered with the God she was missing; he is found hanging on a cross. "For God so loved the world that he gave his one and only Son, that whoever believes in him shall not perish but have eternal life."[10] That's what I said to her. I explained the reason she had lived so long without God. Her guilt both offended him and terrified her. Her sinful will always resisted him and held him at arms' length. But look, there he dies for her, because he loves her anyway. Completely. Eternally. If she trusts him now, one day everything will be what it's supposed to be.

"When you put it like that," she said, "I think I understand."

Not only does the question of this chapter need to be justified, but those who ask it have the obligation to supply their answers as well. Pain is a problem for everyone, not just the Christian. Deny God all you want, the sorrow remains . . . only then it is hopeless sorrow, the suffering is meaningless, and you can't think of one good reason not to give in to despair. (Scrawled repeatedly in the diary of renowned atheist Madalyn Murray O'Hair were the words, "Somebody, somewhere, love me!" Of course. How else could she have felt?) At the end of the day, there really are just two possibilities in a world such as this. There is either eventual terror in a world where anything can happen, a world that is all we have, or there is trust in the unfathomable love, the joy, and the coming dawn of Christ. There are no other alternatives. No halfway house. No middle ground. With tears I ask you, would you think about it again?

The Father you're missing.

The Son dying to redeem us from this guilt and pain.

The Spirit not leaving you alone, even now.

The real heaven that justifies this undeniable longing for home.

"How long, O LORD? Will you forget me forever? . . . How long must I . . . every day have sorrow in my heart?" So wept David, a man after God's own heart, in Psalm 13.

It is sad but true that many people question God out of sheer arrogance and raw unbelief. But, if you're a Christian, do not let your own heart condemn you. There is also a questioning that arises not from unbelief but from faith. It is precisely the fact that you know he is Good and you know he is Right and you know he is Love . . . that your very soul cries, "Then why, dear God!?" And the answer he gives reaches beyond the realm of words and ideas. He gives himself.

The answer is God on a cross, crying "Why?" with the whole world, crying for the whole world from no safe distance away. It is him then standing on the other side of the grave, beaming, "Don't be afraid."

"You're saying God is a man?"

An old woman and a virgin girl visit in the hill country of Judea. That the one should be pregnant and glowing is extremely unlikely. For the other it's impossible. Yet both are. When the women meet, the child in Elizabeth's womb kicks, and Elizabeth bursts out to Mary, "Why am I so favored, that the mother of my Lord should come to me?"

God has a mother?

Fast forward. Listen in on the first recorded conversation of Jesus Christ as an adolescent telling his parents, "You don't understand me." The 12-year-old boy is trying to explain to his mom and stepfather his compulsion to make himself at home, of all places, amid the awesome grandeur of the temple in Jerusalem. What is an otherworldly, strange, and intimidating place to everyone else, to him is . . .

"My Father's house."

Eighteen years later, the quiet life of a carpenter was set aside. Messiah stood in line to be baptized by John. The very skies were torn open, and as the Spirit flew to him, the pride of heaven erupted. The voice of God was heard naming the dripping young man.

"This is my beloved Son."[11]

It seems that those who knew Jesus pondered this one paradox above all. The one sleeping

through a storm—he must have been exhausted—wakes up and tells the storm, "Be still!" The one who stands and sobs at the funeral of a friend—it's only human—shouts at the corpse, "Come out!" Just who *is* this?
    This is the child of Mary.
    The Son of God.
    The Beloved.
    (Please read Luke chapters 1–3.)

There are times in my books when I will ask you, dear reader, to close your eyes, get very still, and ask yourself if the things you're reading aren't true. I'll want you to wonder whether what you're reading about conscience or creation or human nature is something you already know. This isn't one of those times. This is a mystery.
    This is about Jesus.
    What I'm writing about now you won't find written in the stars, engraved on the trees, or whispered to you out of your own innate awareness of God. The answer to this particular question—who *is* Jesus Christ?—can only be revealed by God through his Holy Scriptures. (Later on I'll address excellent questions like "Why believe the Bible?" and even honest complaints like "It doesn't make any sense!") For now, let it be enough for me to explain the biblical teaching about Jesus Christ as clearly as I can.
    Jesus is the eternal, infinite Son of God, without beginning or end. There was "never a time when he was not," as the theologians say. He shares full equality with God the Father and has for all eternity. This sharing did not change when he joined himself with humanity and entered our human story by his conception in the womb of Mary. But through Mary, God the Son became every bit as human as

we are. Imagine. The divine attributes are evident in his stunning life, briefly glimpsed in the stilling of a storm, the reading of a man's thoughts, and so on. However, it was central to his mission that he set aside the full and open use of these attributes. For he came to learn about all things creaturely: quiet pleasures and stabbing joys, everyday headaches and heartaches, and all. He sighed tiredly at the stars from a gazillion miles below and rubbed the calluses on his own right hand. Just like you.

When God the Son came into the world in this way, we refer to it as his "humiliation." Possessing a human nature is not a humbling thing all by itself—Christ still has his human nature, even now in glory inconceivable. No, the humbling part was that during the life he lived on earth, he kept his divine nature hidden within his human flesh, so that he was found in appearance as just a man and nothing more.[12] He looked like, well, just another guy. Even when staggering through a desert starving for food, with Satan taunting, "If you are the Son of God, tell these stones to become bread," Jesus answered, "Man does not live on bread alone."[13] This was Jesus insisting that he experience his time in this world as any real human being does, even the hurt. He came to be the perfect revelation of God in human form. He is a readable translation of the unfathomable Divinity, who was up to something completely new in the universe.

It is an incalculable condescension. Does a man become one of the fish in his aquarium so that, reaching for them, he might see other emotions in them besides fear? Does he yearn to be just one in a million ants that he might thereby communicate with them in fluent Ant?

And yet the comparisons are pale and weak, for in Christ the finite held the infinite, the Uncreated became a creature. God came to be known by us and to show us who our otherwise impenetrable Deity is. The scene of Old Testament people cowering before Holiness at the base of Mount Sinai had its unlikely parallel in boys and girls skipping over to Jesus. Plain folks conversed unafraid with undiminished Deity. And if you want to know how the Author of life felt about death, you only need to watch Jesus at the grave of Lazarus. He wrote the answer on his own human face. You can see how he cried and cried, with tears as weighty with meaning as the miracle that would follow. Or how does the Almighty Creator feel about you, you wonder. Only watch him die. And you know. As Martin Luther said, "We flee the *hidden* God and run to Christ." In Christ the world got its first unhurried gaze into the face of Deity.

"[God] has spoken to us by his Son."[14]

Think about it. Isn't this just what we are aching for? Haven't our hearts been asking for nothing less than this— that God should learn what it means to be here, to be us? And, did he learn! He looked out and took in his own private view of the world, such as it is, from the appalling platform of a first-century crucifixion. For this God came, that he might do the one thing he could not do in heaven. He came *to die*. He was the "Hound of Heaven" that came to look for the lost ones down dark, poisoned alleys, down those "labyrinthine ways,"[15] only because we, having fled so long and so far, would never have found our way back to him.

But, if you would, please fasten your seatbelt so that we can examine the mystery of Jesus' identity in its particulars. Here it goes. The teaching of Scripture is that Jesus is one Person with two natures. Our one Lord Jesus is both completely human and fully divine. And we who are fascinated by Jesus love to speak as accurately as we can about him, as the Word instructs us. Here's the principle: We distinguish these two natures of Christ, but we never separate them, for he is one Person.

1. We distinguish the two natures of Christ. For example, we say that Jesus was able to die according to his human

nature and that he had the power to rise from the dead according to his divine nature. Notice, however, that we do not speak of Jesus as some hybrid mixture of God and man. If he were half God and half man, he would in reality be neither one nor the other. The Scriptures refer to him clearly and plainly as *both* "the man Christ Jesus"[16] *and* "the true God."[17] So we recognize both the human and the divine natures, each distinct, complete, and intact.

2. We never separate his two natures. The mystery is that, though possessing two complete natures, one human and one divine, he is not two different people somehow pasted together. He is only one Person. The same "I" that said, "I am thirsty," is the "I" that said, "I will be with you always." And since he is one Person, one nature is never found apart from the other.

This is the good part, and I'll tell you why. It means that nothing happened to the man, the Galilean, that didn't also happen to God. And there is nothing he does according to his nature as God that he is not also doing as your friend and brother Jesus. I hope I haven't lost you so far. We've taken the long way around to get to the things any child can know.

What it all means, quite simply, is that *God* lived here. And *God* wept. *God* struggled. *God* was nailed to the cross for you. And now I write a mystery. It means that *God* died. And in the darkness of the grave, *God's body* was laid. This is what the Scriptures say: men "crucified the Lord of glory,"[18] and we who believe are the church that "God . . . bought with his own blood."[19]

The Lord was crucified? God has blood?

In Christ he does. Alleluia.

There's more. Who is he who rules the heavens and the earth, who will one day judge the world and all in it? Some unfathomable Deity shrouded in mystery and light? Yes. And also . . . the carpenter's son, the one we saw blessing those children, reaching for a leper, frying up some fish on the shore of Galilee, saying, "Don't be afraid." He is your Jesus. Let the people say, "Amen!"

Martin Luther put it like this. Picture the whole human race on one side of a set of balancing scales. On the other side of the balance, write any wretchedly reasonable heresy about Christ the world has ever invented—that he was one of us and nothing more or that he wasn't really one of us at all—and there we sit on our side of the scale, unmovable, unmoved. But write on the other side of the balance, "The Lord of Glory crucified," and, as Luther put it, *"We fly up."* By faith I fly to the bosom of my Father.

I know who God is, so I know who *I* am as well. The same new name that God uses for his own Glorious Son he also fixes onto you and me for Jesus' sake. This is the mystery. In Christ, we are the ones God loves.

We are . . . *the "beloved."*[20]

If what you've read about Jesus seems wild and strange . . . it is. But you need only remember that it is the strange shape of a particular key that makes it fit a particular lock. The lock is our human need.[21]

We needed a Substitute to live an actual human life in our place and get it right all the ways we always get it wrong. Then we needed him to die a single, human death that would somehow have infinite worth to redeem not just a single life but every life. If death were able to hold him, life would never be ours for sure.

For him to be the One who would lay himself down like a bridge between God and humankind, he would have to really be one of us in every way and, at the same time, infinitely more.

This is the peculiar shape of the lock. The only key is Christ.

"There are many paths to God"

Read again the whispered conversation between a leading Jewish Pharisee and a wonder-working rabbi called Jesus. Ask your questions in this gentle lamplight.

Is Christianity marked by the arrogant pleasure of calling everyone else in the whole world wrong? Not so. To embrace Christianity is to find out how wrong *you* have been from the very start.

Jesus leaned close to Nicodemus, whispering, "Flesh gives birth to flesh." By "flesh" he meant our sinful human condition—not knowing God, not seeing God, neither having any part of God, nor wanting to. In Christianity we find out that we were born that way, bent toward evil from the very start. We learn to be sorry, not only for what we've done, but even more for what we are. You may say you don't care for that. But you can't call it arrogant.

All right, but aren't all religions really the same? Isn't Christianity all about turning our lives around and aiming toward God through strenuous acts of human will?

Far from it. That path, common to other religions, has nothing to do with Christianity. Christian faith means blinking awake to the reality of Jesus, of your Father, of forgiveness, and of heaven, because his own Spirit has given this gift to you. In Jesus' words, it is like being born all over again. No one works or, for that matter, even asks to become alive. No one begs to make his or her own life happen. This is God's work. "The Spirit blows where he will."

Isn't Christianity, when you really get down to it, all about obedience?

Actually, no. It's about love—learning how much of it God's heart can hold. "For God so loved the world that he gave his one and only Son." This is the costly grace that comes down from above, washing over you in the refreshing streams of "water and the Spirit," that is, Holy Baptism. This gift, this love, changes us in all the ways that fearfully straining to obey the rules never could.

Sounds nice, but doesn't Christianity say that Jesus Christ is the *only* way to God? Excuse me, but isn't that rather narrow?

Well . . . um . . . yes, actually. I suppose Christianity *is* rather narrow . . . like a narrow footbridge swaying over a rock canyon . . . like the escape is narrow when the inmate on death row is pardoned just in time. Yes, narrow is precisely what it is.

Like a birth canal.

(Please read John 3:1-21.)

It's a sad joke in a way. The man announces to a semicircle of religious people that he doesn't believe in God. One of them responds, "We insist you tell us, Which God don't you believe in? Allah, Vishnu, or Christ?"

The butt of the joke is the believers, each quarreling to keep his or her own God on top. Aren't we Christians guilty of a compulsion to set *our* path to God apart from all the rest, to exclude every other religion? Don't we demean entire cultures and casually dismiss millions of thoughtful,

educated, next-door people who have truths of their own?
Isn't it the height of arrogance to call our way the only right
way? *Aren't there many paths to God?*

Sadly, we *can* spot cultural arrogance in ourselves—a
superiority based on nothing but being who *we* are, not who
they are—and must be sorry for it. Pride and prejudice are
the things we get from our sinful humanness. They are not
what we learn from Jesus. We need more of Christ, not less.

Notice, however, that Christianity is not merely one culture asserting itself over all others. It is an organic movement as old as history itself, and one that has utterly
transcended culture from its very beginning, to a degree no
other religion has. (And it did so on the winds of grace,
unlike the military conquests that Islam required even to
cross the borders of Arabia.) The Messiah, though born as
the perfect expression and fulfillment of faithful Judaism,
wasted no time transcending his very Jewishness, erasing
every cultural boundary. Two thousand years before Martin
Luther King Jr. intoned, "I have a dream," a Jewish rabbi
revealed the sparkling vision of his own heart to a Roman
centurion. "I say to you that many will come from the east
and the west, and will take their places at the feast with
Abraham, Isaac and Jacob in the kingdom of heaven."[22]

"I see . . . Indians and Africans, Chinese and Finns . . .
gathered at a Hebrew table."

Christ is not the exclusive property of Germans or
Swedes; his inclusive eyes see more than white, middle-class
Americans. The essential Christian faith as I describe
throughout this book wears kimonos and saris, tattoos and
cowboy boots.

Perhaps it is helpful to assure you that being a Christian
doesn't mean saying that every other religion is wrong in
every possible way. The Jewish cleric says that God is One;
the Muslim writings hold that God is holy; the Mormon
elder wants you to live the Golden Rule, and on and on we

might go. When they're right, they're right. There is such a thing as the "natural knowledge of God" that informs the many religions of the world. C. S. Lewis commented that rather than saying all the rest are wrong clean through, we should say that *whatever is true in other religions is perfected and consummated in Christ.*

And yet I must quickly add that the parts of the truth that religions have found by their own natural lights do not include the part that rescues eternally. One vital contradiction between orthodox Christianity and every other faith still remains. It makes all the difference, and I do not attempt to make it palatable to those who disagree. The difference is Jesus Christ. The difference is the way God acted uniquely, decisively, and one time for all to save the whole world. "Salvation is found in no one else, for there is no other name under heaven given to men by which we must be saved."[23]

This is not a bias. I am merely explaining the biblical facts. I do not assume a superior position but the one position that excludes all boasting entirely. It is God, revealed in Jesus his Son and in his phenomenal Word, that is right when the whole world is wrong. And he makes himself clearly known in the broken body of Christ that opened up "a new and living way"[24] to God. There is no other.

A boldly exclusive claim? You bet. However, it isn't much of a challenge to the Christian faith to point out that it claims to have exclusive truth. The same can be said about every possible statement of belief or philosophy. *Anyone* who is trying to say *anything at all* is claiming an exclusive truth that inherently rejects every contradictory statement. "There are many paths to God," for example, is itself an exclusive truth claim that is intolerant to my point of view. It is also the sort of claim that adherents sometimes hold with the most extreme sort of dogmatism in spite of its incoherence. ("Relativism is absolutely true, and we think everyone should believe it." This makes sense?)

Anyway, it is weak thinking to suggest that you should reject a tenet merely because it dares to actually say something. This is how people conveniently refuse to subject their ideas to thoughtful challenge or critical analysis. Doesn't it make more sense that we, on both sides of the religious fence, should learn the art of ethical dialogue, that we should practice a certain kind of talk characterized by "gentleness and respect"?[25] After all, it doesn't require intolerance to claim that Washington D.C. is the nation's only capital. Just so, there's nothing inherently arrogant about quoting Jesus—"No one comes to the Father except through me"[26]—with a humble invitation to explore the quote's veracity together. If Jesus' claim is true, then the compassionate thing is to say so.

"That may be true *for you* . . ." can only strangle with incoherence a good conversation before it begins. The Christian claims either conform to reality or do not. You are free to say one or the other. It is nonsense to say both. The myriad religious paths are mutually contradictory on every worthwhile question—the nature of God, the nature of man, the nature of the bridge between them, or if one exists—and as long as we intend our words to have meanings, we cannot say all paths are equally valid. Open-mindedness to blatant contradiction is not superior to certainty in your hard-won beliefs.

The concern that fuels the many-paths-to-God mentality seems to be that it will be a short jump from disagreements about cherished beliefs to violence and bloodshed. However, no true Christian can take that leap without actually forsaking Christ in that act, nor can any credible Christian leader ever teach the followers of Jesus otherwise. "Ah, but they do all the time!"—is that what you're thinking? Not true. Name a single place in the entire world where people live in fear of the local Christian congregation. Instead, Christians are, in fact, dying every day at the hands of those who believe in other gods. Every day. By most estimates, the number of present-day Christian martyrs exceeds 160,000 per year. Just because of what they believe. Just because of Jesus.

I know this chapter bothers you. It bothers me too to suggest that so many are so wrong. But it doesn't surprise me. Throughout history the masses have nearly always been in error about some fundamental thing. After all, what is it really like when some truth is found? Should we find, for example, a cure for cancer or the precise center of the universe, will it turn out that everybody was right? Will the answer be something bland and vague? Won't it be, in a word, *specific?*[27] So also is the search for God and the cure for sin and death. The answer is as sudden and unexpected—and as specific—as John 3:16.

"For God so loved the world that he gave his one and only Son."

"There are an infinity of angles at which one falls, only one at which one stands,"[28] wrote Chesterton, calling to mind a wooden cross that rises perpendicular to the ground. But what you'll find at that spot is the very opposite of exclusiveness. "For God so loved *the world*." It matters not who you are, what you've done, what color your skin is or what culture you embrace. God loves you. Christ was lifted high to pull your weary head to his chest, your very life into his sweet embrace, whoever you are.

You can choose to exclude yourself, but let's be clear on that point. The only one keeping you out is you. And please, what good is it to stand perpetually at the crossroads, insisting that every option be kept open, never knowing what it is like to run down one path with abandon to the Truth, to him?

When my daughter Abby was born, someone *else* was born at that very moment. A father. It was as if an entirely new person awoke within me that wasn't there before— a "Daddy"—to relate from that moment on to this shiny new little person.

That's what it was like when the God of all grace made an appearance in my life by water and Spirit. I didn't make him come to me. I didn't even ask him. It was all grace. He just showed up. And now there is something new and wide awake in me, kept alive by the power of his own Word, a new "self" turned upward, capable of responding to this Someone New in faith, in love, in worship. I am born again.

"Why should I believe the Bible?"

Picture a seed drying on a sun-baked sidewalk.

Jesus tells a story about a farmer casting seed all around, letting it land wherever—in rocks, in weeds, in soil. For now, notice the kernel that lands on a hard, hard path. Birds come along and snatch it away before anything good can happen at all. If the seed is God's Word, what is this snatching away?

You tell me. Are there things you've heard *about* the Bible that have kept you from hearing what it actually says? Have convenient potshots made the message of God's disturbing holiness and his costly love far too easy to dismiss?

"It's full of discrepancies and contradictions."

"It's nothing but myths and fables."

"It's been proven false by history and archaeology."

Just so many mockingbirds feasting on priceless seed.

Other writers—serious historians, archaeologists, and scientists—have dealt with these objections at length and to the satisfaction of anyone who really wants to know. My purpose is only to chase away the birds long enough for the seed to have a chance. If just once you would set aside the propaganda about the Bible, the half-truths and

lies that many swallow uncritically and repeat unthink-
ingly, what then?

I only want the voice of God to settle once into your soil
like a seed—"I have loved you with an everlasting love; I
have drawn you with lovingkindness."[29] Let it rest a minute
there on the surface of your mind. Turn the ground over
one more time. What might that tiny bit of life become?
Only the faith that saves. The hope that endures.

The love that never dies.

(Please read Matthew 13:1-23.)

Will I now prove the Bible to you? Yes and no, well, sort
of. You see, when the Bible *can* be tested—when the Bible
records historical peoples, places, and events or when it
touches on the nature and experience of humanity—it passes
with flying colors. Yet the really vital thing the Bible says is
different. It is a *spiritual* message that stands beyond the
reaches of empirical proof. It centers on the relationship
with God in Jesus Christ. When I read the Bible, I am confronted by a Person revealing his goodness, bent on breaking my sinful heart, professing his love, and speaking trust
into me. Yes, trust.

This is not to say that a reasonable defense of the Bible is
not possible; it is, on those matters which *can* be tested. I
eagerly invite your close inspection of the biblical data. The
steady integrity of our Scriptures is no Achilles' heel for the
church, the body of Christ. Although I would much rather
talk to you about what the Word of God says, the following
issues may be the ones that seem important to you now, so
let me indulge you.

Go looking for the supposed tangle of contradictions
and be shocked to discover how weak the examples are that

are most often cited—the fact that Abraham told the same lie about Sarah three times does not meet any definition of contradiction I've ever heard. Instead it sounds suspiciously lifelike. Complaints about multiple creation accounts in Genesis, for another example, are failures to grasp the ancient literary style and the rather ingenious (easily demonstrable) literary structure. Recall that the Scriptures were written in a time and place very distant from ours. Step outside of the bias that goes looking for problems, and be stunned at how *few* apparent difficulties there actually are. Although written by some 40 authors over 15 centuries, the Bible presents a perfectly unified treatise of humanity's salvation and a cohesive explanation to the meaning of our existence. *"Men spoke from God as they were carried along by the Holy Spirit."*[30]

Go looking for the myriad contradictory religious opinions that have twisted and changed over time, and be startled by the single Voice that speaks from Genesis to Revelation. Grasp the phenomenon of a book written throughout a period seven times longer than the life of the United States in which hundreds of complex and controversial topics are treated with an essential harmony. Scan the consistent answers to the soul's most persistent questions: Who am I? Why am I here? Who made me? How do I know him? How do I live with him in peace? Find the teachings of the New Testament, supposedly evolved over the centuries (such as the righteousness we have by faith[31] or the physical resurrection of Christ[32]), written with surprising clarity back in the days of Moses and King David. With this the Old Testament falls open as a startlingly Christian book.

The Bible is, in fact, so clear about Christ that even scholars (so often the least prone to take things in a straightforward manner) ought to be able to understand. The words of Job ought to take our breath away: "I know that my

Redeemer lives, and that in the end he will stand upon the earth. And after my skin has been destroyed, yet in my flesh I will see God; I myself will see him with my own eyes—I, and not another. How my heart yearns within me!"[33]

Listen closely as a single theme recurs in book after book, whether written by a king of 1000 B.C or by a physician 1,100 years later. Some 40 writers collaborated across the centuries on a single fascinating story. What consumed them all is Christ.

"These are the Scriptures that testify about me,"[34] he said.

When someone says, "Who knows what the original says?" go and examine for yourself the more than five thousand pieces of manuscript evidence for the New Testament alone—a measure of support that utterly eclipses the evidence for any other ancient writing, not to mention the more recent works of Shakespeare. Consider that, based on five pieces of manuscript evidence, no one bothers to question whether we can know what Aristotle really taught. Indeed professors of classical antiquity salivate over the overwhelming mountain of documentary evidence at the heart of Christian scholarship and, frankly, think that liberal religious scholars who suggest otherwise are nuts.[35]

"Heaven and earth will pass away, but my words will never pass away."[36]

Or perhaps you've heard the old saw that the biblical documents that have come to us as copies of copies are shrouded in uncertainty as to the original words. There is a serious science of textual criticism that, by comparing copies from all around the ancient world, convincingly assures anyone who is listening that not one iota of Christian teaching is in doubt due to conflicting readings. Investigate for yourself the painstaking care of the Old Testament copyists and the extreme measures they took to verify their work, such as counting the occurrences of letters and discarding entire copies if their number of letters didn't match the original's.

This constancy of the Bible texts through the passing centuries is what the fuss of the Dead Sea Scrolls is all about. From a manuscript one thousand years older than those previously available, came a symbolic handshake from centuries past, promising that nothing of consequence was lost to time or tampering. The texts we read today do not differ in any substantial way from those fresh off the authors' hands.

"The grass withers and the flowers fall, but the word of our God stands forever."[37]

Others try to inject doubt based on the issue of *canonicity*—how do we know which ancient writings belong in the category of authoritative Scripture? The church did not so much *decide* which documents belong in the Scripture as *recognize* those that had the credentials. Does a given document belong to the set of Old Testament writings—"the Law of Moses, the prophets and the Psalms" (Luke 24:44)—that Jesus clearly affirmed? Is a candidate for inclusion in the New Testament an authentic work of an apostle and witness of Christ? Does a document speak with that common spirit of the entire body of Scripture? These are issues of scholarly objectivity, and historic Christianity has provided exhaustive, disciplined, and satisfactory answers. No one could have prevented the actual words of God from becoming the canon of Scripture. The writings that were divinely inspired rose to the surface of the sea of human words *by their own power . . .* as surely as the music of J. S. Bach could be trusted to distinguish itself from the pile of music I myself have tried to write.

"My sheep listen to my voice,"[38] called the inimitable Shepherd.

Press those unbelieving scholars for the real reason they handle the Bible as they do—ridiculously elevating other sources above the Scriptures, spinning ingenious theories about its formation without a scintilla of evidence—and it becomes clear. The Bible conflicts with their worldviews. That's the reason. There is no other. If you listen closely to the simplistic attacks people make on the Bible's credibility, you may just find yourself persuaded to my point of view by the sheer emptiness of their arguments.

"This is the verdict: Light has come into the world, but men loved darkness."[39]

So the God of the Bible seems to think he has the right to destroy human life? He's not *playing* God. He *is* God. Do not evaluate him as if he is a mere human being like us. Humble yourself before the One who not only created human life in the first place but has the ability to *re*create it, that is, to resurrect it on the Last Day and render upon it a righteous verdict. You may complain about how the Bible so vividly demonstrates that there is such a thing as God's wrath; you may fret about the psychological discomfort such a demonstration causes people. I only ask which is the greater danger, to believe in God's justice . . . or *not* to? Open your eyes to the world in which you live and to the damage and pain that comes precisely from those people who do not believe in eternal consequences to the awful things they do. Let us not conveniently forget what happens when antitheism weds to political theory and social engineering—mourn the *one hundred million* killed by communism so far. The Bible's messages of God's holiness and his love are precisely what the world most needs.

"Be still, and know that I am God."[40]

You may try to dismiss the Old Testament Scriptures as the nationalistic writings of the Israelites, like those of any other ancient people. But first, for the sake of your own integrity, read for yourself the carefully documented history that is unique for its unblushing, brutal honesty about the nation's own persistent moral failures and those of its greatest lights— Abraham, Moses, and David. It is inconceivable that such a history was fabricated. Similarly, you may call the New Testament an invention written with a religious bias to benefit an emerging church. Discover instead the same unblinking frankness about the church's own pillars, detailing Peter's rashness and Thomas' doubts, John's temper and Paul's crimes. "Christ Jesus came into the world to save sinners—*of whom I am the worst*"[41] is not the sort of thing you make up. And I remind you again of the unimpeachable character the entire New Testament has. The Scripture named its witnesses and disseminated its accounts within a time frame that allowed for testing and contradiction by its opponents.

"That which was from the beginning . . . which we have seen with our eyes, which we have looked at and our hands have touched—this we proclaim concerning the Word of life."[42]

When someone claims the Christian "myth" has been exploded by archaeology, ask if they're aware what the archaeologists themselves are saying about this Book and how its historic reliability is more and more *taken for granted.*[43] Why not sift through the 25,000 archaeological sites that show connections with accounts of the Bible?[44] Myths do not concern actual people and places! Ask about the ruins of Jericho, where the walls have collapsed outward, and compare the ruins to Joshua chapter 6. Ask about the Pool of Bethesda, which was found just where John said it would be in chapter 5 of his gospel. The truth is, modern visitors to lands of the Bible cannot help but come away impressed with the real geographic and historical backdrop of the biblical text. The underpinnings of negative biblical criticism are themselves pre-archaeological. They were all advanced before the utter vindication of the existence of written language in Abraham's day, the dating of John's gospel, the impeccability of Luke's history of the life of Jesus, and the birth of the church (to name just a few of a hundred examples). No historical statement of the Bible has been proven false by archaeological research.[45]

"We did not follow cleverly invented stories when we told you about the power and coming of our Lord Jesus Christ, but we were eyewitnesses of his majesty."[46]

Is the Bible just a collection of religious writings like many others? The phenomenon of prophecy can persuade otherwise. Hundreds of prophesies of Christ written in the Old Testament came true in the New with incredibly precise detail and against staggering odds. A few close calls by the likes of Nostradamus, culled from endless pages of bad guesses, don't hold a candle to the perfect prophecies of God. Always right. Never wrong. Let the hairs on your arms stand up as you read for yourself—read just once with an unresisting mind—the prophetic clarity of Psalm 22 or 69, or Isaiah 53.

"Jesus took the Twelve aside and told them, 'We are going up to Jerusalem, and everything that is written by the prophets about the Son of Man will be fulfilled.' "[47]

There is no dispute about the uniqueness of the claim the Bible makes for itself as the very words of God, intoning hundreds of times, "This is what the Lord says;" about its unique endorsement by the one truly unique Man, Jesus Christ; or about its unique dissemination to the ends of the earth, according to the audacious prediction of our Lord.

"And this gospel of the kingdom will be preached in the whole world."[48]

Do you assume there are other writings of antiquity with similar qualifications? I answer, without fear of contradiction, that every single one of these credentials is unique to the Bible. The Koran makes no prophetic gambles. The Hindu Veda can only exempt itself from the test of contradiction. The Book of Mormon lacks so much as a single, corroborating piece of a broken clay pot. There you have it; go and find another book like the Bible.

You'll find instead the worn-out hammers lying broken beside a pristine anvil, the divinely accented Word. It uniquely has survived centuries of vicious verse-by-verse assaults. Gone are all those who have attacked it, while the so-called myth remains, outliving its adversaries and defenders as well. Each dated denial becomes passé and passes away, revealing itself as the myth and shadow before the solid, living Voice of the Lord.

And here, at last, is the point. There is no great leap of faith when it comes to believing the Bible. To listen and follow is not to take an unthinking step off a high, dark ledge. The Voice behind the Scriptures has never lied to you. You may find ten thousand things in the Word of God that, when tested, turn out to be absolutely true. This Word tells you things *about you* that will resound within you again and again, if you'll only listen.

So then, when it matters the most, when you read the one other thing that stands outside the arena of physical evidence—the transforming love of Christ expressed in his own crucifixion—that love asks for no leap . . . only a falling into someone's arms. *"I have loved you with an everlasting love."*[49]

This is your relationship to God, its beginning and end. "I love you," he says in Christ by his Word. You answer, "I know."

And now, to draw closer to the Word . . . is to draw closer *to him*. There is no difference. To hold tightly, in a dark night of soul, to one of his promises . . . is to hold tightly *to him*. To make room in your mind for this seed to quietly grow, to save a place for it . . . is to save a space for him.

"Isn't religion discredited by science?"

Which came first, the chicken or the egg?

What makes that question so intriguing is the difficulty of imagining either a chicken that didn't come from an egg or an egg that didn't come from a chicken. So you come to this rather startling conclusion, once you think about it, that you have to look outside the sequence of chickens and eggs to explain them.

A similar problem, only miles deeper, involves the human body and the genetic code imprinted on every cell within it, that fabulously intricate instruction manual called DNA. The only thing that can conceivably make this miraculous stuff is the human body, and the only natural way there can be a human body is if there is first DNA. It's the ultimate chicken-and-egg mystery. We have two things of stupefying complexity—the human body and human DNA—and neither one seems possible if the other wasn't there first.

That's the barest glimmer of the marvel of you and me.

And you are not to let anyone rob the wonder away, not even if it's someone holding a test tube with the aura of science all about. We were specially created by God, our Maker. We were knit together in the wombs of our mothers, where Deity saw our unformed bodies and wrote all our days in his book before any of them came to be. That's right. God. You have to look beyond the sequence of DNA and the human body—you must search outside the sequence of birth and death—to explain us.

You have to look up.

You must follow the gaze of the Man from Galilee, who alone has the right and the authority to speak on the matter of our existence.

In Matthew chapter 5 we find Jesus sitting on the side of a mountain, teaching his disciples, pulling back the veil, sharing his timeless secrets. He expounds the cloudless worldview of the One who made the world. Sit and rest and listen to the unwavering voice, asking us to consider them again, the lilies of the field, and to see how the Father helps them with their clothes.

"Look at the birds of the air. . . . your heavenly Father feeds them. Are you not much more valuable than they? . . . O you of little faith."

(Please read Matthew 6:25-34.)

Let me quickly assure you that I won't take an extreme position in this chapter. The point will be to suggest an honest approach to science that will allow you to "oooh" and "ahhh" over the latest scientific discoveries with the rest of us. Go ahead and blend with mine your hushed "thank you" to scientific research for the medicines that keep loved ones alive. Wonder at the technological achievements that make your life so very comfortable. At the same time, please know that in every generation before ours, there were people who brought a healthy skepticism to the very latest and most self-assured decrees of science. Especially when science meandered into philosophy, ethics, or theology, when it pontificated beyond its own expertise, those who questioned were right to.

Have you heard about the pamphlet published in 1852 titled *Ten Scientific Facts That Clearly Contradict the Bible?* Not a single "fact" is still taken seriously today. There's an important point to be made here. Some people think the conflict between science and faith goes back to the days of Galileo, whom the church ignorantly condemned for saying that the earth was not the center of the universe. "See," they gleefully say, "the church should have listened more closely to science." But in truth it was the mathematician and astronomer Ptolemy who had told the church that the earth was at the center in the first place. The church's problem was that it *did* listen to science. What science said . . . well . . . it kept changing. Today's new science will, with certainty, be smirked at tomorrow. I'm not the only one who thinks so.

In his intellectual landmark *The Structure of Scientific Revolutions,* Harvard nuclear physicist and historian of science Thomas Kuhn reveals scientific consensus to be a sea of shifting sand. The history of science, objectively observed, demolishes the notion that the best science of any generation can ever approach truth with certainty. Here's what scientific progress is really like: a community of practitioners forms under the umbrella of a *paradigm,* a governing point of view that, for a time, seems best to fit the facts and wins the intellectual field. Institutions are founded on that model, careers are made, textbooks are written, and theories (in name only) harden unnoticeably into concrete fact. But then that paradigm, unquestioningly embraced by a generation, painfully and inevitably gives way to another. Inevitably!

Here's how it happens. An anomaly is observed. Some new phenomenon appears, and no matter how the standing theory's box is stretched and pulled and modified, the problematic fact refuses to fit inside it, creating a crisis in the scientific community. Eventually, the old theory, so colossal and far-reaching and seemingly invincible, cannot be sustained any longer. It comes crashing under its own weight. And at last a new idea, a new theory, a new paradigm emerges and takes hold—one that both explains the data originally gathered and one that could have predicted the anomaly as well.

"And this time we're really, *really* certain," say the folks in the lab coats.

It is not science's fault that the puzzles of such apparent simplicities as light and gravity, energy and matter are simply beyond humanity's full grasp. As Albert Einstein said, "The universe is not merely more complicated than we can understand. It's more complicated *than we can imagine.*" All I'm saying is that before you go pinning your personal philosophy to the most recent dogmatic certainties of science, you need to realize that they will be gone tomorrow. Please see science as it really is: the composite work of countless human beings meshing facts with hunches, advancing imaginative ideas with interpretive observations, celebrating successes and hiding errors, baring their biases in the face of opposing points of view, and now and then losing all objectivity. (Witness the faithful clinging to Darwin with no factual support. Watch the shoulders shrug over the fossil record that steadfastly refuses to say what it's supposed to. Perceive the determination not to let a divine foot in the door in the straight-faced theory that aliens must have seeded life on this planet.) Or is it somehow a slam on scientists to say that they are really a lot like the rest of us?

Speaking of healthy skepticism, there are just a few things I don't get. One is how scientists can be confused about whether light is made up of particles or waves, yet be certain it is uncreated . . . and continue to speak as if the case against faith is self-evident. What I don't understand is why by knowing the laws governing the formation of raindrops, we would know that God does not form them. (We don't know that about rain, by the way, and still it falls on the "righteous and the unrighteous."[50]) And I don't see how life ever ushered itself in, how that squirrel named Chance ever scrambled across the million-lane highway in front of it.

I fail to grasp what is so unreasonable about believing that God made the world, this lone island of life in the blue universe, with an aspect of age. Children like to ask whether Adam and Eve had belly buttons, signs of a babyhood they never had. Sounds silly. But you see, in Christian theology the earth *has* a belly button, that is, it was created as a mature world, bearing the apparent signs of a history it never experienced. What would have taken a stupendous stretch of time if we would have had to wait for it to happen by itself—take the pinpoints of light flickering from the other end of space or the stunning extravagance of life-forms on this planet—all came to be in the span of a week at the speaking of simple, creative words. This fact alone will forever confound any sort of science that proceeds from naturalistic assumptions. As Martin Luther once said, "A slight error at the beginning becomes very great at the end." What then if the error at the beginning, at the level of prior assumptions, is colossal?

Here we hit the essential issue: assumptions. Let me be honest about my own presuppositions in the hopes that you will be honest about yours. I simply believe that divine revelation is an immeasurably more reliable way of knowing the fundamental truths of our existence than is scientific investigation. Divine revelation is the Christian *epistemology*—how we know what we know. God reveals his Truth in his Word. The human lens has proved itself to be cracked and blurry, flawed and limited, and destined to futility. This is shown when the human search for truth invents its own starting points, when human thought is no longer tethered to the "natural knowledge of God," when reason cuts itself loose from the awareness of the Divine that comes naturally to us all through conscience and the awed contemplation of nature.

I live by faith, you see. My assumption is that if science were ever to scale the mountain of ignorance (by asking of nature the right questions and rightly reading its signs), as the members of the heroic community topped the last rise and ascended to the highest peak, they would find that a classroom of Sunday school children had reached it first—boys and girls at their verses.

"And God said, 'Let there be light.' "[51]

It would be a mistake for me to move the argument this book is making from the "Thus saith the LORD" of the Bible to the "Here's what we now know" of even the most brilliant and well-meaning human authorities. In my mind, should I appeal to the numerous underreported findings of science that could support creationism, for example, even if I win the point, I surrender too much. I will have silently conceded that the real reason I know I am right is that some folks with Ph.D.s in quantum physics agree with me. But that is not the reason at all. I refrain from making the hesitant glance in their direction. I give up the passion to avoid sounding stupid, and I cheerfully make my confession of faith in the God who fashions the snowflakes. I won't even concede that the Bible is true in spiritual issues and is only mistaken in matters of biology or botany or astronomy. The Bible makes no such distinction. You see, my belief is simply not anchored to prevailing scientific theory, and it certainly is not tied to the pious, amateur "Christian science" from a previous generation. My confession dangles miraculously in midair, held only by the hand of God. Any attempt to buttress God's revelation with human thinking only diminishes his revelation and obscures the mystery and marvel of it.

"By faith we understand that the universe was formed at God's command."[52]

By faith. Allow one more analogy, a very personal one. If you brought me evidence of my bride's unfaithfulness, I don't care what it is, I would still know that I could trust her, for reasons having nothing to do with the weight of the seeming evidence against her. Some spouses, you say, do turn out to be unfaithful? Yes, but some spouses deserve to be trusted far *more* than they are, regardless of how things may seem for a time. Just so, I trust God is faithful. That is my assumption. I trust him. But not blindly, as you suppose.

I now direct your eyes to the single, greatest anomaly in the long history of a predictably dying humanity, to the stubborn aberration, the event that *had no right to happen.* I refer to the resurrection of Jesus Christ from the dead. I know that it happened, and I accept all of its earth-shattering ramifications, every single one. I throw my head back and laugh as I think of every thought that needs to be *re*thought when one has visited ancient Jerusalem. There it is.

I leave it to the scientists to discover where they went wrong. The resurrection of Jesus is the real thing, the once-for-all-time thing that would not bend down for the test of repeatable experimentation. I worship the Anomaly, the Christ, and let the intellectual chips fall where they may. The minds that resist the miracle are themselves both miracles and fools. Let every fact obediently follow; let every theory dash its head against this rock if it has no room for Truth. He lives.

And there follows an entire worldview, whole and complete—the way things look from atop the hill shaped like a skull. You are authored by God, fashioned and made. You are also a fallen thing, rebelling against your very Life. But he came for the love of you. He died to call you forgiven. Only trust him, and because he lives, you will too. It is his desire to hold you as his own, to sustain your faith against the world's enlightened condescension, by his own Word. And it is his plan someday to come and take you home.

Call it the God-so-loved-the-world view—the one that successfully predicted such fundamental issues of your existence as meaning and mystery and wonder—the one with answers to such ubiquities as guilt and fear and death. To see this view is to see how much is at stake in this matter of science versus faith. Where do we come from after all? Ponder a line from journalist Steve Turner: "If chance be the Father of all flesh, disaster is his rainbow in the sky, and when you hear State of Emergency! Sniper Kills Ten! Troops on Rampage! Whites go Looting! Bomb Blasts School! It is but the sound of man worshipping his maker."[53]

Is it so? Or do we come from—and is the way open to return to—the Love, the very essence of God, and the Truth that were at the founding of the universe? So says the Word of God. We come unavoidably back to the real issue. Who are you going to believe?

The Creator thundered from his cloud to the questioning mind of Job: "Brace yourself like a man; I will question you, and you shall answer me. Where were you when I laid the earth's foundation?"[54]

Appropriately humbled by those stirring words (again), I listen skeptically to the world's talk concerning the great puzzle of our existence. A baby girl nuzzles her head against my shoulder, warm puffs of air tickling my neck. And I, a true radical now, remember the humbling beauty of the cosmos and the vast spaces of knowing that the world's theories leave out, and I wonder what I did to deserve lapping water or Canada geese, the color blue or middle C. "If you can't touch it, smell it, kick it, enter its measure into a column, it doesn't exist," some like to say. But I inch closer to the puzzle's Creator as he whispers his pleasures into my ear: "Consider how the lilies grow . . ."[55]

Cling to today's science if you will, but it will be old tomorrow. My God is forever young, never tired, still delighting in the glorious repetitions of the wonderful world he has made. "[His mercies] are new every morning; great is your faithfulness."[56] As the sun dares to rise golden above another day, I can almost hear the silent whisper of Christ.

"Again."[57]

"I can't handle your outdated view of sex"

It started out as small talk about water and thirst. (They were sitting by a well.) But without warning, the conversation turned a sudden corner.

"Go, call your husband," instructed Jesus.

"I have no husband."

"I know."

And he pulled back her bandage, revealing the five ugly wounds beneath.

That's how often she had married, how many men had promised to her and to God that they would always be there for her . . . and how many times she had wound up alone. Well, she wouldn't let *that* happen again. Instead, she lived with number six, giving away her body and soul, no longer bothering about another promise from yet another man.

And so, the conversation was about being thirsty after all, being dreadfully parched for something she had never once found. And though she quickly changed the subject and led the conversation away from her own history as far as she could take it, this was not necessarily a bad sign. She was not so far gone that she no longer felt her shame.

She scrambled out of this painful light, throwing out a diversionary complaint about religion. Her final feeble evasion in the end had a curiously modern ring. It was her last ditch attempt to shake loose. She said: "Messiah is coming. He'll explain everything."

In other words, "Whatever."

But as he had done from the start, he gripped her with his words and held her, refusing to let her go: "I who speak to you am he."

It was not merely that he *has* everything her heart knew how to want.

But that he *is*.

(Please read John 4:4-26.)

On the matter of human sexuality, aren't Christians hopelessly out of touch? No, I don't believe so. If I told you not to steal candy bars, would you ask me, "What do you have against candy bars?" Would it occur to you that it might just be stealing that I am against?[58] You see, there's an idea spooking around in the world that the Christian church is somehow against people having sex. Much the opposite, only Christianity properly elevates human sexuality, sanctifies it behind plush velvet cords, and bothers to whisper a hushed thank you to God for its wonderful, creative powers.

It's stealing that Christians are against.

And I don't only refer to robbing the pleasures of sex under those circumstances in which they are neither ours to have nor is it safe to take them. I refer to what we say about our very bodies themselves. The ancient wisdom declared that when we call our bodies our own to do with as we please, this is precisely where we err. "You are not your own; you were bought at a price. Therefore honor God with your body."[59]

"You are not your own."

His audience was a standing-room-only crowd of college students. Stephen Covey was trying to make the case for the existence of objective standards of morality, in particular, sexual morality. He claimed that there exist certain "true north principles," independent of our shifting opinions, that we each carry within ourselves in that "compass" known as the conscience. Well, the college students weren't buying his claim, and he knew it.

Their objections were intelligent, articulate, and vehement. Realizing he was getting nowhere, he paused and calmly asked them if they would just close their eyes and get completely quiet. He asked them only to contemplate what he had been saying about sexual morality, to contemplate that there is such a thing as objective standards. If, after two minutes of inward reflection, they were still convinced he was all wrong, he said that he would just give up, walk out the door, and leave them alone. They agreed. When they opened their eyes two minutes later, something had changed. To their credit, those college students were honest enough to admit that, well, they suddenly weren't so sure.

It is that same kind of quiet that I depend on as I make the same appeal *to what you already know.* I only ask you to consider the following about human sexuality and to ask yourself, "Is it not so?" I'll call it The Plan. Have you somehow never noticed it?

By "The Plan" I mean the way a woman's body is perfectly designed for a man's, and his for hers. And the fact that out of such an intensely rich and pleasurable experience— a way for one person to thoroughly enjoy another—comes the miracle of a child. (Yes, *miracle.* No other word will do.) And if man and woman only kept that gift of sexuality sacred, if they only let it be the bond it was meant to be between the two of them alone, if they only protected this holy pleasure behind the hallowed walls of a lifelong promise—"as long as I live, you'll never be alone"—what would be the result?

Just for starters, the child they create would always have them, Mommy and Daddy. Every child would. There would be no little one with a "daddy-shaped hole" in his or her heart; no woman raising a child alone under the shadow of shame that, try as she might, she can't talk out of her heart; no teenage girl with her heart torn out and her future in ruins because she played with fire; no teenage boy waking out of the dream of safe sex to a nightmare reality called AIDS. None of that.

With a bit of that little thing called self-control, upon which any happy and worthwhile life depends, these people could create families, thanking God for what he's made them and living in his smile. And you could look at a father looking at a mother and a mother looking at her baby and begin to penetrate the nature of God.

> "Can a mother forget the baby at her breast
>   and have no compassion on the child she has borne?
> Though she may forget,
>   I will not forget you!"[60]

The Plan: the heartbreaking, sweet glimpse of the way things are *supposed* to be. And I ask you, is this plan not as beautiful as it is self-evident? When it comes to sexuality, do you thirst for anything less than this? Do you really yearn for nothing more than someone else's body? Perhaps in this quiet you can begin to detect society's cynicism when it doesn't want to acknowledge any such thing as a plan, when it calls naïve and inexperienced anyone who does, when it resents the very suggestion that there is a way things are supposed to be, when it is busy making plans of its own. Can you not see the sickness in our culture so consumed with sex? A person who divorces sexuality from its beautiful purposes within marriage and for procreation is not unlike a bulimic person who gorges on food and then vomits; each wants mere animal pleasure but refuses human nourishment. Our culture is anything but enlightened and sophisticated when it comes to sexuality.

The Christian apologist Gilbert K. Chesterton compared complaining that a man can only marry one woman to complaining that the Garden of Eden only had one entrance or that a man only gets to be born once. You see, it's a profound *in*sensitivity to the magic and miracle of human sexuality, a failure to comprehend its lovely power to bond two people for life, that treats it so casually and so cheaply. And I ask, is it even possible that you do not see the pain, destruction, and human wreckage left in the wake of sexual promiscuity?

But why don't you see these things? Have you confused sex for a far deeper desire? Have you settled for the merely physical pleasures—have you become driven and enslaved by them—when what you are actually thirsty for is one real relationship? But follow the thirst even further than that. Do you perceive in yourself an emptiness that nothing in this world satisfies, for which no human love could ever be the answer, for which there is only the passionate devotion of God himself?

"I have loved you with an everlasting love."[61]

What is this ache, this dull, persistent pain you would push away at all cost? Do you dare to ask? Has your need to feel better for a little while—the need that made you reach for any satisfaction you could find—only taken you further and further away from Love?

We are not to be condemned for being thirsty. This is human. But heaven itself looks down and shudders at the ugly places our thirst takes us—everywhere but to God, who alone is the "water" that matches our yawning need.[62] It is not merely that the plan and the beautiful, blessed lives we were supposed to enjoy lie in shambles at our feet. No, the truth is worse than that. We have not sinned against a plan, but the Planner. Inspired by the arts in their less-than-finest hours and caught in the spell cast by ten thousand movies and popular songs, we believe the message daily smuggled past our defenses, that sex on our own terms is our one happiness, our reason, our life.

And we treat God as less than nothing.

This is the cost of our immorality. We have made ourselves insensitive *to him*, whose every intention was to bless us. We have offended that very One we need and long for, have scrambled out of the presence of him who is our life, and have poured into the ground the only water that could have ever satisfied us. Is this not so? Is this not the self-evident truth begging to be let in? Have not our very bodies filled up with sin? Are we not without excuse? Yes, but don't be afraid.

"You are not your own; you were bought at a price."

She was caught in the act of adultery, dragged into the street, exposed to the world in a hateful act. If you don't see it that way, you would if you were married to the man she slept with. You would feel the outrage. She should not have done it. And her partner, having used her, should not have let her face the music alone while hypocritical men gathered to condemn her. None of this, not one bit of it, was The Plan.

Then along came a rabbi named Jesus. The men confronted him. They wanted to know if the immoral woman should be stoned. He crouched down to write something in the dirt. Was it their names? Was it their sins? We don't know, but we do hear the sound of stones thudding into dust, when the only Real Man she had ever met stood up for her.

"If any of you is without sin, let him be the first to throw a stone at her."

And with that Jesus and the woman were left alone in the middle of the street. Then he said something to her, sudden and unexpected: "Neither do I condemn you." And grace, like water, flowed to the lowest part.

Because there was *another Plan,* an ancient mystery older than the hills, hidden in God's heart for ages upon ages. This rabbi would die in a way he never deserved. He would be condemned for her, and us. This was the price.

And his "Go now and leave your life of sin" was not the sound of a last-second rebuke but of a prison door swinging open. She was released. There was a way back to the life she was made for. There was such a thing as a real, true relationship. There was such a thing as love.

"I have a mind, and this doesn't make sense"

An argument broke out among the disciples as they walked along the road, an argument about who was the greatest in the kingdom of God. Jesus motioned to a little child and had him stand up small in the midst of all those childish grown-ups. "Unless you change and become like little children, you will never enter the kingdom of heaven."

As you study Jesus in the gospels, this is the one elegant thought that brought him deepest pleasure. He would lift his face to heaven just to say, "Thank you, Father," when it came into his mind. This is the thought: God has hidden his best things from the cleverest and the most talented and has opened his beautiful presents in the presence of children.

And I ask you to think about it. What if God does just that? What if it is simply God's pleasure—if it just broadens that smile at the center of all things—not to hide his deepest things on the top shelf where only the smartest and brightest can find them? What if he places them instead on the bottom shelf—down low, shoved to the back—where only the humble or the child can ever really reach them? What if it is God's delight to whisper his best secrets into the lowly, contrite heart? What if the

truth behind all that we see—and the answer to everything wrong here—isn't found through a brainteaser
requiring us to be smart but through a Person asking us
to trust him?

Then the greatest in the kingdom would not be an
Albert Einstein or a Stephen Hawkins but . . . well . . . one
of my little girls . . . singing "Jesus Loves Me" in the back-
seat as we drive along the road.

The path of human reason is one that keeps splitting
and splitting and then splitting again. When our most brilliant minds hold opposite truths, either most of them are
wrong or they all are. But among them stands one who is
unique. It's Jesus, holding up a little one and smiling:
"Whoever humbles himself like this child is the greatest in
the kingdom of heaven."

(Please read Mark 9:33-37 and Matthew 18:1-4.)

So the Christian message is an offense to your logic? God
called for a *human sacrifice?* And the sacrifice was *himself?*
Isn't it all just a little, how shall I say it, absurd?

So "Jesus saves" is a jarring, strange-shaped thought that
can't be made to fit inside your orderly, no-nonsense mind?
Rather than dare to paper over the difficulty, I will let you
know that God himself says, "I know how it sounds."

"The message of the cross is foolishness to those who are
perishing. . . . Where is the wise man? Where is the scholar?
Where is the philosopher of this age? Has not God made
foolish the wisdom of the world?"[63]

I maintain with the apostle Paul that God sounding
foolish is wiser than anyone else sounding brilliant. The
man on the cross in the middle is God come to die in our
place? You want to say that no intelligent person could ever
swallow that? Just as salvation was accomplished with

ancient miracles, witness the modern miracle that God
is, in fact, able to keep such salvation, with its seemingly
mythical radiance, in the thinking of so great a mass of
human beings. What refuses to work on paper works quite
well in the simplicity of the believer's life. Millions of
intelligent, thinking people do take it all as fact. Left to
themselves and their own best reasoning, none of them
ever would.

And those who turn away, scoffing empty scoffs, are
themselves fulfillment of prophecy: "Look, he is coming
with the clouds, and every eye will see him, even those who
pierced him; and all the peoples of the earth will mourn
because of him."[64]

But before you misunderstand me, I want to assure you
that I'm not asking you just to "toss your mind out the
window," as they say. I'm a Christian, but I wasn't born
again yesterday. Our ability to think is a gift from God.
Reason's noble purposes include scientifically investigating
this wild, curious universe and solving what problems it
can. I'm only asking you to consider how human reason by
itself, if you mean it to be the path to ultimate truth, has
certain problems.

If you deny God on the basis of human thought, it
is actually thought that shrinks to nothing, not God. Let
me explain. If God is removed from the picture, then
human thinking itself is just another accidental product of
a pointless evolution. Why, then, should it be trusted? After
all, when we know what *causes* a person's thoughts—*he*
only thinks that way because of his environment; *she* just
thinks that way because of her genes—we declare those
thoughts invalid. Therefore, if human thinking itself were a
blindly determined product of a meaningless, evolving universe, there is no reason that it, of all things, should be
meaningful. Yet another argument against faith self-
destructs when human ingenuity raises its stubby fist

toward its own Creator. Ironically, the fruits of scientific invention that we all enjoy today could have only grown on the tree of a Judeo-Christian worldview, the worldview that insists that the universe itself is orderly, meaningful, and, therefore, a fitting playground for rational investigation and scientific discovery.

There is nothing illogical about merely recognizing logic's limitations and sometimes exercising other muscles besides raw intellect. We all know this. To use reason to comfort a child or to write a poem or to win love *would be un*reason*able*. There is more to us than barren intellect. A mind without a heart is a hopeless amputation.

Consider the conclusions reached by some of our brightest and best. There are those much smarter than I who are concerned, on philosophical grounds, that they do not actually exist. Descartes' "I think, therefore I am" helps people to hope that they are not actually figments of their own imagination. Other people, called solipsists, believe they do exist but nothing and no one *else* does. I confess that they arrive at such places by paths of philosophical argumentation more ingenious than I, for one, can entirely follow. Does that make them right? Those who say things like these ought to say nothing further, for words themselves should be meaningless to them. Logic pitted against God always winds up playing the fool. Always.

It reminds me of a situation described by Chesterton in which a paranoid-delusional man is convinced that the entire world is out to get him. Chesterton explains that the problem with that man is not that he has lost his mind but that he has lost everything *but* his mind. The thing to notice is that his belief *makes sense logically*. Any evidence you might offer that there is no such conspiracy against him becomes "just what he would expect you to say" if the world *were* a giant plot against him. The interesting thing about his paranoia is that he's exactly right.

His delusion is impenetrable by rational thought. He has the whole thing completely reasoned out to his own satisfaction. In this way, his belief is just like those philosophical ideas I've mentioned above, such as being skeptical about existence itself. Reason has brought otherwise reasonable people to those absurd places, and therefore, no amount of further reasoning can set them free. Regarding that paranoid man, Chesterton points out that for that poor, logic-bound mind, the only hope would not be found in more logic but in a window that is thrown open within his tight circle of invincible reasoning.

Perhaps a certain humility is the fresh air he needs: "You are *not* the center of everything. The whole world is not about you. You are *not* all there is." It is just that humility that *we* need, that clear-thinking, sound-minded meekness of Job: "Surely I spoke of things I did not understand, things too wonderful for me to know."[65]

The simple truth is that God exists in "unapproachable light,"[66] far beyond the short arms of puny logic. "As the heavens are higher than the earth, so are my ways higher than your ways and my thoughts than your thoughts."[67] Human reason, as an instrument, is not only finite but also damaged, along with everything else in this world. God is unknowable and unreachable by the best of human thought—like the sunset to a person born blind, only more so. If we were to know him at all, God needed to reveal himself by his own Word.

We come at last to the very highest purpose of these miraculous minds of ours. Human reason is an indispensable gift, being the organ that allows us to know and relate to God as he speaks to us in his Word and we seize his meaning. Mental abilities are required for grasping the truth being communicated in the Holy Scriptures. But then, rather than allow reason to sit in judgment on the revealed truth, it is our place to simply believe—this we do by a power not from us—and let the alleluias form in our minds.

Thus Martin Luther thought of reason as "the handmaiden of theology" or, if you like, logic is like a janitor in an art museum. Though the janitor's role is indispensable, there are treasures in those halls that are far too precious for the "janitor" to be allowed to handle, things too wonderful and alive for logic to be allowed to vivisect. Though our minds throw up objections to God's Word, *"we take captive every thought . . . to Christ."*[68] Though created logic wants to tear down its own Creator, faith interrupts.

"Shhhhhh," it whispers, "God is speaking." What is he saying?

"God so loved the world that he gave his one and only Son . . ."[69]

For we are the ancient Israelites all over again. With our backs to the water and with angry, glinting Egyptians bearing down hard on us, the only safe path was the impossible one . . . through the middle of the sea. *Be still and wait for the glory of the Lord.*

The result of recognizing the Word as a thing more trustworthy than our own thoughts, as something that is right when everything else is wrong, is not confusion but stillness, mental wholesomeness, and assurance—the only kind I have ever found. God declares himself close, not to the brilliant mind but to the broken heart that still whispers, "I am sorry." Then, ah then, the love of Christ crucified is like blazing sunlight. If you can handle, so to speak, this one mystery that is too brilliant for human eyes to see directly into, then by this light everything else becomes suddenly crystal clear. As for me, "My heart is not proud, O LORD, my eyes are not haughty; I do not concern myself with . . . things too wonderful for me. But I have stilled and quieted my soul; like a weaned child with its mother, like a weaned child is my soul within me."[70]

The peace that surpasses all human understanding, like a holy wind breathing past our open windows, keeps watch over our hearts and minds in Christ Jesus.

C. S. Lewis pointed out that it is not a difficult thing at all to imagine circumstances that require faith, plain faith, in the faces of things that don't seem to make sense. There are any number of times we might ask someone to trust us even though we sound completely illogical. To follow you farther up the ledge is the way to get safely down? The puppy's paw must be pushed farther into the trap for us to get it out?

The only proof to offer is the look in your eyes. It's all the scared child or whining puppy can understand. Indeed, in real life it can make sense to trust what doesn't seem to make sense, especially when it's all we have.

Here in the dark, dear Jesus, the only Light is you.

"Don't you condemn homosexuals?"

"This man of no reputation loved the weak with relentless affection, and he loved all those poor in spirit just as they were. He was a man of no reputation."

So wrote the late Rich Mullins in the one song during which he was afraid he would end up sobbing instead of singing. His "man of no reputation," of course, is Jesus, the Friend of sinners. That's the smear of the self-righteous that Christ wore like a badge of honor. They tried to insult him with "He eats with prostitutes and sinners," only to hear something like: "Bingo! They're the reason I've come!"

"Not for the healthy but for the sick."

"Not to condemn the world but to save the world."

And so it happened, as Christian author Philip Yancey pointed out, that when God himself showed up in the world, the main complaint people had was that he wasn't "religious" enough. The lost ones gathered around him finding warmth and welcome while the "respectable" ones coldly looked on. But please don't misunderstand. Though Jesus loved them as they were—adulterers and sinners—it was not as though they could remain the way they were. None of us can. Forgiveness is not only a free gift; it also holds the power to change us in the ways that we want to change if we know God at all.

Although we don't have a record of Jesus encountering homosexuals, we can be absolutely sure of one thing. If any persons were poor in spirit—if they brought to Christ their empty-handedness, their brokenness, their "you-must-change-me-because-I-cannot-change-myself" dependence—they were treated to a sort of grace otherwise unknown in the world. They learned that God, in Christ, would not hold their sins against them.

Those poor in spirit learned that they didn't have to keep degrading themselves, not anymore. They learned the tenderness and the power that all sinners can always get back to.

"For this I have come."

(Please read Matthew 9:9-13.)

I won't forget the tenderhearted woman I saw being powerfully drawn into the Christian faith. Her one overwhelming concern had to do with homosexuality. Her problem was that she likes people, and one or two of the people closest to her happen to be gay. Her biggest fear about Christianity was that she might be put in a position where she would be expected to be harsh, condemning, even cruel to these people whom she cares about very much. So many challenging questions . . . finally an easy one. "Love them," I said. "This is first. You must understand that neither the Christian faith nor Christ himself will ever ask you to do anything but love them."

Of course, the demands of love go far beyond holding pleasant feelings for them. Love means willing and acting in their best interests, whatever the cost. This is what she and I needed to talk about next. What is in the best interest for homosexuals? What does genuine love for them look like? First, it doesn't mean that we display our revulsion for this one sin in particular, as if other sins, take our own for example, are of a more respectable kind. Among the things that disgust us ought to be the hypocrisy of people treating homosexuals hatefully while giving not a second thought to their own heterosexual immorality. "First take the plank out of your own eye,"[71] said Jesus, not so that we would make no moral judgments at all but that we would see clearly when we do. Yes, homosexuality is a serious sin, deadly serious, but that doesn't yet distinguish it from other sins. If you want to insist on putting sinners into categories, there's only one distinction that really matters: Some sinners repent. Others do not.

That's why the frightening thing about homosexuality, as with other sexual sins, is how often it becomes an expression of willful defiance against the will of God. The time to be most afraid for the gay person you care about is if no thoughts about Christ ever spoil the pleasure of his or her sins, if he or she no longer struggles against it, regrets it, or prays that things were otherwise. That is to say, his or her particular sin has hardened into a chosen lifestyle where no room is left for "God, I'm sorry. I reject what I've done. You must help me." You see there *are* people, spiritually alive people, who struggle with their homosexual temptations in the same way I struggle with my own. I brush the snakes off my legs. . . . Or else I am sorry when I do not. I receive my forgiveness. I move on in the grace of Christ, sighing my prayer to become more like him, hungry to demonstrate that my repentance has been sincere. Many who live with homosexual temptation do this as well.

Homosexuals have sexual desires that are plainly unnatural. Simple biology says so. All psychobabble about repression aside, they must realize they simply cannot act on these desires. These desires must be rejected outright. I don't mean to offer an offensive comparison between homosexuality and pedophilia except to make a single point no one can dispute: Certain people in this difficult world feel strong sexual desires that are of such a kind that they simply must be resisted. (By the way, would it matter if a "pedophilia gene" were identified? I would like to think we would still call that behavior abhorrent.)

That homosexuals cannot marry makes them no different than people who cannot marry for other reasons. I don't say that lightly. Many people carry heavy burdens, and this may be theirs. Yet, in carrying it through Christ, they could find unanticipated spiritual gain. They must die to themselves and their unholy desires so that, in the love of Christ, they may be alive to God. In my own way, so must I.

What is the godly, loving attitude to have toward homosexuals who *don't* resist their inclinations? Love them as you love yourself. That is, regret their sin and explain precisely why you do so. Tell them that you are sad that such an awful thing should be loose in them and that you continue to care what happens to them. All this you do—please notice this—in just the same way you regret and are deeply saddened by the ugliness of your own sin and still pray for your own good. Let them know all this. While you wait for their godly sorrow, preview for them the forgiveness and grace you are aching to speak to them.

"If you were only sorry, truly sorry, do you know what I could tell you then?"

Meanwhile, when responsibilities at work or in your personal life bring you into contact with homosexuals, treat them with decency and human-kindness so that you can be there someday to pick up the pieces with them. And by all means, pray there *will* be pieces; pray that the lives they are living so far from God will fall apart before it's too late. God's Word is clear—unrepentant homosexuals will die forever.[72]

One important quality for remaining available to them involves being more quick to spot—and more deeply bothered by—the things you see *in yourself* than the things you see in them. Your own forgiveness by God himself through Christ is an unfathomable wonder. Don't forget it. Be glad just to slip in among the "tax collector and sinners" that gather around Jesus and to have a place of your own among the rest of the lost and found ones. If you cultivate these attitudes of humility and grace, you'll be in the best position there can be to say things to people that they do not want to hear. In my experience, it makes all the difference. Homosexuals who see hatred in other people's eyes every single day will notice the difference they see in yours.

I suppose what I'm asking you in all of this is, Have you ever cried for them? I mean, for homosexuals. It has been documented that one cause of the fierce temptations they experience can be the horror of childhood sexual abuse. Such things should not have happened to them! And cases of homosexuality stemming from such a cause cannot possibly be wholesome and good. I have personally dealt with the devastated families from which homosexual sons or daughters, mothers or fathers were led away like slaves, wearing a single, defining desire like a chain about their necks. I cannot easily forget the sad resignation in everyones' eyes.

No matter what the circumstances, homosexuality isn't a very promising lifestyle. What's wrong with homosexuals—and we all have something wrong with us—happens to be especially painful. They are likely to be social outcasts even today, too familiar with cruelty, rejection, and profound relational wounds. They can create no children of their own—just one more joy they miss. Speaking of children, there is no evidence to suggest that it is in the best interest of kids to be raised by practicing homosexuals. There is, however, evidence that those children are more likely to experiment sexually. Most of all, homosexuals can only raise children on top of the tragedy of those very children being without either a fully present mother or father. (That other tragic situations cause the same aberration and the same inevitable heartache is a poor justification.) Theirs can never be a situation without the sin and sorrow built in. My Jesus grieves over them. Do you?

And on top of all that, the societal message homosexuals constantly hear, the one that they think liberates them, is keeping them bound. The message is "This is what you are. There is no other way for you. Accept it." The truth is there are people being released from their slavery to homosexuality every day. I'm not suggesting it's an easy path—far from it—but the simple truth is that there are methods of intervention that have been successful in enabling gay people to lead God-pleasing lives. Evidence suggests that for some homosexuals, longings for affection from their parent of the same sex became confused and entangled with their sexuality very early in life, way back behind their earliest memories. On that premise, people are being healed through older counselors of the same gender who offer mature, affectionate, strong, and godly love.

Call all this hate if you must, but I answer that you do not know my heart. To have the mind of Christ is to desire your highest good. That is why I write as I do. The alarming anger that gays-turned-straight encounter from the gay community reminds me of people in Jesus' day who wanted to kill Lazarus *for the crime of being raised to life.* The new lives that former homosexuals are now enjoying in God-pleasing heterosexual relationships call the worldview of the activist gay community a mistake and a lie.

More important, there are seven New Testament words that breathe life and hope into the struggling homosexual who feels helpless and compelled to surrender outright to this sin. The news is good. The apostle Paul clearly listed homosexuality among the sins that plague human beings and ruin relationships with God. But then the sentence ends in a breathtaking phrase, that is, if you have ever cried for the lost ones: "That is what some of you were."[73] Such were some of you. Homosexual is what you *were*. Not anymore.

Like Jesus, given the choice between the hypocritically self-righteous and the poor in spirit, I'll take the poor in spirit any day. How privileged I am when I get to speak to the sorry ones of Christ. For there is one who "love[s] the weak with relentless affection," who was not ashamed to be touched by former prostitutes or to take his meals with the likes of broken sinners like me. Like you.

Come as you are to the man of no reputation.

"Your amazing grace just seems too easy"

Another standing-room-only day in the life of Christ. A crowd clogged every conceivable entrance of the house while he preached inside. Outside, a circle of friends surveyed the scene. One of them was paralyzed and needed desperately to be seen by Jesus. So love found a way.

Imagine the wonderful commotion, the delightful mess. Dirt and debris fell all around. Dusty shafts of light stole through the ceiling, together with useless, mumbled apologies. These outrageous friends tore an opening in the roof to lower the paralytic down into that makeshift sanctuary. A lesser man than Jesus would have been outraged at the disruption. He glanced up at four heads decorating the skylight. "Jesus saw their faith." Wasting no time, he looked down at the object of such affection, the mumbled, useless man, and saw the Need behind the need.

"Take heart, son; your sins are forgiven."

Now, some who were watching had a problem with this. Their minds loudly grumbled the word *blasphemy* with logic that was simple and valid. It is the one sinned *against* who gets to say who is forgiven and who is not. But don't miss Jesus' implication:

"All your sins—against Goodness, against Love, against God—were sins against me."

Their private complaints—"Who does he think he is!"—were transparent to Christ. His reply was quite simply brilliant.

"Which is easier: to say, 'Your sins are forgiven,' or to say, 'Get up and walk'"?

Notice that the question wasn't which was easier *to do*—to forgive or to heal—but which was easier *to say*. The answer, of course, was "You are forgiven." Any mouth can make a claim about the mysteries in God's heart. But once Jesus would say, "Get up and walk," the whole house would know whether he had the right to say it, whether his words were a cruelty or a scarcely imaginable power. Do you see? Jesus bound up for all time his ability to heal people's bodies with this authority to pardon their souls. If he could do the one, the other could no longer be denied. "So that you may know that the Son of Man has authority on earth to forgive sins . . ." he announced. Then, lowering his compassionate gaze to the man on the floor, he said, "Get up!"

No one could breathe. They leaned forward, mesmerized. This beautiful pause held the hope of the entire world. If the man was able just to climb up those words and to reach his own full height, then what else was true? His sins were forgiven, of course. And by the way, so are yours. Get up . . . get up . . . get up.

He got up.

Now turn it around. What if Jesus had not asked, "Which is easier to say?" but "Which is easier *to do,* heal a man's body or forgive his soul?" That's a different question altogether. For that we would need to compare the effortlessness of Jesus' miracles to a long, slow crucifixion. Ask the questions: Is forgiveness easy to accomplish? Were we so easy to love? Was it a walk in the park to save me? They take us to a different place entirely . . . an awful place. . . .

A place not even easy to *look* at.

(Please read Matthew 9:1-8.)

With this chapter, I roll any number of objections into one:

"*Salvation?* I say it's 'deeds not creeds.' Surely God values what people actually do over what they happen to *believe*. Will he ignore all the wrong you've done, Christian, then punish me for mere incredulity?"

"*The gospel?* It seems a strange notion—completely unjust in fact—that God should punish his innocent Son and declare sinners not guilty. It doesn't seem right."

"*Forgiveness?* If it comes unearned, as you say, what is to keep people from doing whatever they want? Don't tell me some people don't think that way. They do."

"*Peace with God?* You don't know what I've done. It's too late for me. I'm no good. God may pardon those who deserve it, but not me."

"*Grace?* There's no free lunch. No one has ever given me anything. I've worked hard all my life, and I've earned everything I've ever gotten."

Whether you're a philosopher or ethicist or homespun moralist—whether you identify with the messed-up prodigal son or his self-righteous brother (the one who never, ever, *ever* messed up)—you have the same problem with mercy. You sit there blinking at the scandalous love and at the embarrassment of just-like-that forgiveness. You find you cannot swallow the Christian gospel, as much as you might like to. It's all just too easy!

Now there's a perfectly fine answer to all these objections, but only humility can ever make sense of it. Someone has commented that only two things have ever truly changed the human soul. One of them is sin, a far greater problem than we tend to realize. If you only recognize sin's reality, its consequences and its power, you can capture some small sense of how repellent it must appear to an unspoiled God. If you're with me so far, the rest should be . . . well . . . easy. If there were to be any such thing as salvation, it would be God's own doing or it wouldn't be done; it would come as a gift or not at all. It has to be free because, frankly, we have absolutely nothing with which to purchase it for ourselves.

You see, sin renders us incapable of performing the sort of works our God has the right to demand. *He is unutterably holy.* Do we impress him by doing a little good to other people, getting around now and then to what is simply our duty? He is *Goodness personified.* Do we put God in our debt by managing to do fewer of the self-centered acts he despises? He is *incomparably Righteous.* Just what did we think we were going to give to God that would erase the bitter fragrance of all our disobedience when even the disgraces of a lifetime ago are still *now* to him? He is *eternal God.* The fact that our efforts to curry his favor are fearful, guilty, and mercenary spoils everything from the start, because these qualities exclude genuine love for God. We slide our measly bribes a few inches across his infinite table. The currency of our dead works is worthless. He is *the righteous Judge, the Sacred Perfection, the offended Lord.*

And "all our righteous acts are like filthy rags."[74]

What it is like to recognize these truths may be described in many ways. *Easy* is not one of them. And it was not easy to save us. Not even for God. "During the days of Jesus' life on earth, he offered up prayers and petitions *with loud cries and tears.* . . ."[75] He also "*suffered* when he was tempted."[76] He resisted sin and knew its full force. In just the same way, the power of a river is felt by the man who dares to stand against it, not by the man who floats along with its current. Jesus Christ accepted every costly obligation of perfect truth and goodness and consistently denied himself every illegitimate comfort. In this unkind, unholy place, this was a single perfect life painfully pieced together out of an infinity of flawless moments. And, in a word, it hurt—to say nothing of the dragging of a crossbeam upon a torn-open back through stony Jerusalem toward a skull-shaped hill. To speak of "deserving" or "not deserving" such a thing is to misunderstand the words. *Forgiveness, mercy, grace*—these are precisely the words you use when deserving is no longer in the picture at all. As Jesus himself said of salvation, "With man this is impossible, but with God all things are possible."[77] Love found a way.

We were loved before we were born, saved before we even sinned. Before we started out on this journey, he already saw us home. So what is the second thing, besides sin, that changed the human soul? It is this grace of God. Yes, Divinity was willing to take the risk that some would be left unaffected by grace, whether they call it a lie or merely pretend when they call it the truth. But if there is anything that has ever had power to shake the soul's foundation, create its own opening, and plant something new, it is the words of Christ. He was willing to die for the right to say to them:

"Take heart, son. Your sins are forgiven."

"Well, if forgiveness comes freely, can I just go do whatever I want?" Now I'm smiling. Please notice that this is one objection that only the faithful witness of Christ ever has to confront. If you're asking it now, I'll take it to mean that I have presented God's grace in the same spirit as did the apostles of Christ, who were compelled to answer this very question. Listening to the Muslim, the Jew, or the Hindu, this thought will never occur to you. Sadly, it won't often come to mind even as you sit in the worship houses of many Christian denominations. Only the shocking grace as articulated by the likes of Paul, Peter, and John could give rise to such a query: "Shall we go on sinning so that grace may increase?"[78]

Step a little closer, and the answer is clear: "By no means!"[79] God forbid that grace should be cheapened in such a way, that it should be taken, of all things, as a reason *to be bad!* Those whose hearts were once broken see in grace a powerful reason to be good, to love, to praise, to walk in the footsteps of Jesus. And, no, *easy* is not the right word to describe this either. As it was for him, so it will be for us. After all, the Christian church on earth emulates the life of Christ in his humiliation, not his exaltation. The glory is yet to come. First the cross, then the crown.

"We must go through many hardships to enter the kingdom of God."[80]

May I return to an interesting word from the story of Jesus and the paralyzed man? What did they mean by accusing Jesus of *blasphemy?* To *blaspheme* is to *take something away* from the awesome Lord of the universe, to whom all glory and honor rightfully belong. It is blasphemy to snatch away from God one of his privileges, to claim to have a right only God has, or to diminish with words, if that were possible, his awesome qualities. When the people at the house thought the forgiveness of Christ was blasphemy, they had it all wrong. Blasphemy is in those who fail to ascribe to God the qualities that bring comfort and inexpressible joy. Blasphemy is in those who would snatch away from God his right to "have mercy on whom I have mercy."[81]

Fullness and joy consist of precisely this, that you take nothing away from Jesus. Not his power. Not his sacrifice. Not his tender, eternal embrace. And not his right to speak his words.

"Take heart. Your sins are forgiven."

There's an instructive moment in Victor Hugo's *Les Miserables.* The scene begins with a dreadful abuse of kindness. Jean Valjean has been caught stealing silver from the old priest who took him in. He is dragged back to face the shame and consequences. A loud knock by the arresting officers arouses the cleric. He sees and instantly understands.

"I am glad to see you. Well, but how is this? I gave you the candlesticks too." The cleric retrieves them and places them in Valjean's hands. The man of God then leans forward and whispers, "Do not forget." From that moment on, *Les Mis* is the story of a cold, calculating man utterly changed by the only thing that ever could change him. The act of the cleric worked its power on Valjean precisely because it was free, unexpected, unasked for, unearned. It was, in a word, *grace,* the sort that unavoidably calls to mind Christ and his own parting imperative.

"Remember me."

"I'll deal

with

all this

later"

During Jesus' ministry among us, many people stood face-to-face with the Giver himself. Because they couldn't see the road ahead as well as they thought they could, some politely said to the Grace standing before them, "Later." The unsettling thing is how legitimate their reasons sound.

From one it was: "You go on. I'll catch up. I just want to say good-bye to my family."

From another: "I need to go bury my father. After that, you'll see me."

Being the nice people we are, we might have answered them: "Of course. It can wait that long. You go do what you need to do."

"Let the dead bury their own dead," said Jesus.

It's a disturbing answer . . . until you discern the sorrow. The eyes of Christ follow as each disappears around a bend. See what he sees.

"You're going to miss me."

Jesus understands this business of inventing distractions. He once spun a parable about it. In the story, a wedding banquet stands for the kingdom of heaven. Though we could spend forever begging to be let into God's gracious presence, the parable portrays God as the one who begs us. He invites and invites . . . then invites again.

"Come to the feast."

"Uh . . . I just got married . . . just bought a field . . . a brand new ox," people say. "I have all these things to do . . . these front-row tickets . . . this new set of clubs." In other words, "Later."

They fail to grasp that the opportunity to follow the gracious call of Christ comes in a quick passing moment called now. You can say, "Later," but don't think for an instant that you can measure the cost.

Those who walked away from Christ might have glimpsed the self-sacrifice of the Lord of life on the wood he himself carried. They might have witnessed a grave become the place of ultimate hope and Mary offer worship at the temple of his risen body. There is such surprise and joy waiting at the celebration of the very Son of glory himself. And the wedding banquet never ends.

It outlasts their ox . . . their marriage . . . even the very field they walk upon.

But they aren't there.

They missed him.

(Please read Luke 9:57-62 and 14:15-24.)

There are many variations on the "I'll deal with all this *later*" theme. Here are some examples:

"I just don't feel any need for religion right now. This is my time to enjoy my life, pursue my happiness, and have my fun."

"What you say may be true enough, but you have no idea how *busy* I am."

"The heart wants what it wants. I'll do what I'm going to do. *I'll repent later.*"

Let's talk about these examples in order. You aren't interested in religion? You feel no particular need for the very

One in whom "we live and move and have our being"?[82] That doesn't alarm you just a little bit? Might this complacency about life's largest issue be itself something of a need? You live as you must not live, as though God does not exist. How can that be safe? Besides, to be a Christian is to lose, in a manner of speaking, any interest in "religion." The Christian's interest is in Christ.

But you say you are enjoying your time too much to spend it on God's things—reading the Bible, praying, sitting in church? It isn't surprising that you think these things would take too much time away from your fun. It's clear that you see God himself as a taker. Didn't Jesus say, "Any of you who does not give up *everything he has* cannot be my disciple"?[83] He would rob you of your pleasant distractions, your Sunday morning quiet, your forbidden thrills, and give precious little in return. Whatever this grace is that Christians talk about, perhaps you'll be willing to endure it when you're old and used up. Is that what you think?

It doesn't occur to you that the God of all that you see might have something to give you, that the bitter sacrifice of all your hangovers and meaningless sex could be a good thing. You think God wants to take your fun. You don't understand that there exists no pleasure that God himself did not think up for your happiness. Satan has never invented a single pleasure. He only tricks you into *stealing* the beautiful things that God himself would freely give you in his own time and in his own way. Satan wants to steal *you* from God and from the only possibility of joy that lasts. The momentary gratification Satan offers is the price he will gladly pay for the unholy gratification of devouring you for always, until long after these pleasures have turned to dust.

I think I see your problem. You just don't *know* God yet, or grace. In the stolen pleasures and the stiff drinks—it takes a little more than it used to, doesn't it?—and in the new experiences and the new people—for it always has to be something new—you're still trying to find joy outside of God. You still think there is such a thing. You don't realize that even the partial enjoyment of God that is available now in this world is better than the full enjoyment of anything else. The Lord whispers, "Come to me, all you who are weary.[84]

"When you sin, come to me sorry. When you fall, only fall on me. Carry around a word of mine always in your mind. Come to me. Know me. Follow me."

You answer, "Later."

This is you saying something loud and clear, directly into the face of God: "You don't look good to me." How long do you plan to keep saying this?

And what about how busy you are? You are living the ultimate and most tragic example of the "tyranny of the urgent." That telling phrase describes the thousand pressing things on your list of goals and to-dos. Their "tyranny" is the way they all shriek, "Do me *now*." They crowd out the other things in your life that don't *seem* to carry that sense of immediacy: your health, your family, and, most of all, your Lord. These "other things" can always be pushed off to another time. Yet they matter the most, and you know they do, even as they settle mutely at the bottom of list after list after list. And in the evening, in a million American homes, this conversation is heard:

"What's on tonight?"

"Oh, that? I've seen that."

And still they watch, spending that portion of their lives neither on what they should nor even on what they enjoy.

No time to seek the face of God? No time? It seems you've forgotten what time is and what it is for. You ignore the glistening opportunities that arrive with the sun every day. "I have loved you with an everlasting love," says the timeless One. This life is your time to give him everything—

your sin, your shame, your fear, your death—to hear and believe his grace, to draw near and bow down.

Realize that some things you may do with your time matter more than other things, to a degree you can scarcely imagine.

Fifteen minutes of unrushed devotion at the break of each day.

An hour of worship at the opening of your week.

A 20-second absolution from a new Christian friend.

A 20-minute sermon on the meaning of grace.

Sixty seconds to receive Jesus' body and blood.

These are small snatches of time that have an impact on eternity. This is you finding out that there is *another point of view*. Your life is a time of grace. "Follow me" is the winsome invitation of your Lord, who is dying to be heard over the din of the deceptively urgent.

Yet I admit the third version of "Later" is the most unsettling. You say, "I can repent later." I answer, "But *will* you?" You have no good reason to think so. "I'll repent later" is what "Bill" said to me after he had left his wife and son. The conversation is etched on my mind; it includes my plaintive reply: "Bill, will God's Spirit be anywhere in you as you take up with another woman? What will become of this new faith you've found? If you are able to do this now, how hard will your heart be a year from now or after ten years of pushing God away, shutting out the thought of him and deliberately forgetting his grieving Spirit?" The "change of mind" Christians call repentance is a gift that the Spirit of God works in us by his Word. You cannot change your mind without him, which means that repentance will not happen whenever *you* decide you're good and ready.

Ultimately, the answer to all three versions of "Later, Lord" is the same. Jesus is set before you at this moment, not another—"We urge you not to receive God's grace in vain. . . . I tell you, *now* is the time of God's favor, *now* is the day of salvation.[85] God, who lives beyond the realm of minutes and millennia, past and future, nevertheless drags his holy finger across the time line of your life in this fading world. He is always found in the moment of that touch, the present. You can only find him or know him in the now. Yesterday is a frozen river, and tomorrow dangles always just out of reach. Receive the grace of God now. Do it quickly. Trust in Christ while there's still time.

Do you know when your eternity is scheduled to begin? "You fool!" God says in another of Jesus' stories, "This very night your life will be demanded from you."[86] You wonder, who needs Christianity when life is going just fine? But what you do not see is how none of your distractions will mean anything in a hundred years, or ten thousand—not your box seats, not your golf game, not the whole world you gained in exchange for your soul.

There will only be you either with him or without him, forever.

What is the kingdom of God like? In the wisdom of the Christ-Teacher, it takes metaphor and story to get anywhere near it. The kingdom of heaven is like . . . like the wedding banquet of the precious Son . . . like a father's arms wrapped tightly around a prodigal son . . . like a shepherd traipsing over hill after hill in search of a single lamb.

And it is like this. It is like the man who found treasure buried in a field. When he found it, he knew just what to do: "In his joy . . . [he] sold all he had and bought that field."[87]

To see Jesus at all is to catch a glimpse of something priceless. To be in your right mind is to waste not another second in making Jesus yours, whatever the cost, and to let nothing, I mean nothing, keep you from making him your firm possession.

"I believe in reincarnation"

In one of Jesus' parables, we meet a rich man in fine linens of luxurious purple. Whatever philosophy this rich man holds is one that encourages him to ignore the misery at his very doorstep. That's where a poor man, Lazarus, lies starving, crawling with disease. Not surprisingly, Lazarus dies.

Some people would say it is right to let the poor man be. He is working out his karma, receiving punishment in precise measure for all the evil of his past lives. Why should anyone interfere?

In Christ's point of view, it is an awful thing that this poor man is left alone to suffer.

Well, the rich man dies too—no surprise there either—and it turns out that the afterlife holds a staggering reversal of fortunes. Poor Lazarus flies to the bosom of father Abraham and to everlasting bliss in the presence of God. The rich man enters eternal torment, such that a drop of water would seem a relief.

Notice that in Jesus' story, as in all the Scriptures, heaven and hell are not stopovers for the traveling soul known as *eckankar.* They are final destinations. No one leaves these places. No one crosses over from one to the other. There is no reincarnation, no dreary succession of lives lived in this world as the soul strains to get it right. No soul is ever just blown out like a candle—the meaning of *nirvana*—even if one wants to be.

Back to the story. Hoping to get a warning to his brothers, the rich man in hell wishes that Lazarus might be given another life on earth. Certainly, a man back from the dead would have the power to warn the rich man's brothers about judgment and convince them it is so.

This is where the parable comes to its point. First of all, what can God possibly give people that is more certain than his very own Word? The rich man and his brothers refused the Word. Second, people who don't want their time of purple and fine linens disrupted would have no trouble denying a little thing like a resurrection from the dead.

As always, Jesus knows what he's talking about.

(Please read Luke 16:19-31.)

I need to be clear that my purpose is not to ridicule anyone else's belief.

However, it becomes necessary to distinguish Western Christianity from Eastern mysticism, which utterly contradicts Western Christianity because of how common it has become to find the two blurred together. Disciplines such as yoga and mind-blanking meditation and concepts such as eckankar, karma, nirvana, and reincarnation are nowadays dressed up with Christian imagery and vocabulary. Yet the result is not a mixture at all. What remains is still entirely Eastern mysticism with nothing truly Christian remaining. The above parable of Jesus is enough to point out the vast and fixed gulf between East and West.

That gulf is very real. By its own admission, Eastern religion has tenets that are hopelessly self-contradicting, but its philosophy is defended in the name of the mystical way of thinking called Both/And. Though two beliefs are mutually exclusive—there is a God and there is *not* a God—it is considered a higher kind of enlightenment to perceive that *both* the one *and* the other are true. Meanwhile, Western thinking remains muddled in the Either/Or and cannot possibly understand the thinking of the East. Really? An American-turned-Hindu laughably accused a Christian named Ravi Zecharias, "You just don't understand Eastern thinking." (Zecharias was born and raised in India.) The conversation that ensued was quite entertaining: "So you are saying that *either* Both/And thinking is valid *or* Either/Or is, but not both. Do I have that right?" Finally the American caught on that Either/Or thinking was continually asserting itself in his every attempt to prove that Eastern Both/And thinking makes any sense. It doesn't.

This doesn't prevent Americans from finding a strange appeal in this or that Eastern idea, most notably, the idea of reincarnation. In the movie *Patch Adams,* the title character, played by Robin Williams, has his grief over his girlfriend's suicide relieved when a butterfly flutters by. It's her. He just knows it. A really nice result of such a selfish and tragic act as her suicide, wouldn't you agree?

It's not only "nice" but it's also typical of beliefs formed in our Western culture. Western culture takes what seems most pleasing from Eastern mysticism, such as reincarnation with its fresh starts and second chances, and leaves the distasteful parts alone. The less-appealing side of Hinduism includes the Hindu hells to which even Dante's inferno can't hold a candle. Then there is that crushing teaching of Eastern perfectionism, as perfectionism must always be felt in the end by imperfect people like us. The abject poverty, rigid castes, starving masses, and unchecked diseases of India are not only unrelieved by the beliefs that were born there but in certain ways are made worse by them.

Most telling of all is the fact that the concept of reincarnation that people in our culture find so appealing is anything but appealing to people in the East who actually understand it. Fresh starts and second chances are precisely what reincarnation is *not*. Instead it is a dismal sentence to a seemingly endless succession of punishments in life after life after life, as souls suffer for pasts they aren't aware of and can learn nothing from. Existence is a dreary, spinning wheel, and people would give anything if they could only *get off* the wheel. Reincarnation is not nice at all. In fact, enter the gurus, those spiritual guides whose sole purpose is to help people possess enough "enlightenment" to somehow escape the maddening cycle.

There are other problems with the notion of reincarnation. Simply put, there is no continuity between me and some butterfly that hatches after I die. There is no common essence between an insect and a human being—nothing an insect can possess that would be in any sense *me*. Further, the evidence for reincarnation is purely anecdotal. It rests solely on the weird happenings that people report. Frankly, there's no experience so fantastic that you can't find someone who says it really happened to him or her. Even if it could be documented that someone possesses intimate knowledge of a past life, this is still evidence waiting to be interpreted. It would not mean that reincarnation is true. You see, the Bible says there are lying and deceiving spirits in the world, and these certainly do possess knowledge of past lives. Therefore, a woman's apparent memory of her life in ancient Egypt does not offer any significant challenge to Christian theology or any reason whatsoever to abandon the truth of God's Word. This woman is being deceived.

The Word of God is an authority far higher than human intuition—"it just sounds right to me." It plainly trumps human experience—"it felt so real." In God's clear Word, we read that it is given to a person to *"die once,* and after that to face judgment."[88] But thank God, this is not all his Word has to say!

> "But you, Bethlehem Ephrathah,
>   though you are small among the clans of Judah,
> out of you will come for me
>   one who will be ruler over Israel,
> whose origins are from of old,
>   from ancient times."[89]

Five hundred years before Christ, the prophet Micah knew what Christians now mean by *Bethlehem* and knew that the origins of the one born there were, literally, *"from days of eternity."* Dubious evidence of reincarnations based on knowledge of past experiences is nothing compared to evidence of biblical prophets who saw God's own incarnation *in advance.*

"Therefore the Lord himself will give you a sign: The virgin will be with child and will give birth to a son, and will call him Immanuel."[90]

It turns out the universe has a door. Of all the billions of lives that have ever been lived, there is one life to pay attention to—the life of *Immanuel,* "God with Us." God himself fully shared our humanity, not primarily to raise our consciousness (though he certainly does in his way) but to offer his splendid life as a sacrifice of atonement. This is not Buddha under a lotus tree, denying reality, claiming that pain isn't real and that you can think it away. This is God on a cross, *embracing* our pain and death, searching the sky with his eyes, crying "My God, my God, why have you forsaken me?"[91] He did these things in our place, for all our evil, leaving absolutely nothing left over for us to work out in regard to our eternal bliss.

And so the child in Sunday school represents all the "enlightenment" there really is. She already possesses all the universe holds for her when she believes in Jesus, her Savior. To call our God the God of second chances is nice but doesn't go far enough. *"As far as the east is from the west,* so far has he removed our transgressions from us."[92] (Did you catch that? If you were to go north in a straight line and travel far enough, soon you would start going south again. But east and west never meet. Not ever.)

When Jesus the Son of God died and rose from the dead, it meant salvation was finished for all of humankind. By faith in him, he is born again in us. The secret to life and the path into peace is not to empty the mind but to fill it *with the Word of Christ.* In this way, he invades this world all over again, revealing himself in the compassion and love his mysterious presence stirs up in the ordinary Christian. When you're hurting and someone comes along who might help you, you might want to pray that it's someone who is learning from the Teacher, Jesus Christ, not a traditional, disinterested guru.

Here is one last measure of the space between the East and the West: the Christian faith is not dedicated to the avoidance of all suffering. There is sin and sadness here. Even the exquisite sunset holds a silent sorrow to break your heart . . . because it ends. Yet the pain in this life is not to be denied but entered and felt for the gifts it has to give. God is always at work, through Word and sacrament, keeping his children awake to that new and deeper dream, the one that is fully alive in the wreckage of every shattered hope for the here and now. That truer dream is simply to know Christ the Son of God, to reflect him well by the power he gives you, and to see his face forever. The sorrow and pain now only puts you in touch with this dream and in touch with the fact that it's all you've ever really wanted. Soon, very soon, by the merits of Jesus our Savior, we will be together in glory.

And, friends, it doesn't end.

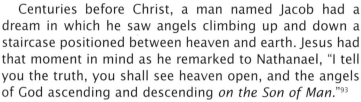

Centuries before Christ, a man named Jacob had a dream in which he saw angels climbing up and down a staircase positioned between heaven and earth. Jesus had that moment in mind as he remarked to Nathanael, "I tell you the truth, you shall see heaven open, and the angels of God ascending and descending *on the Son of Man.*"[93]

"You'll see that the angels ascend up and down . . . *on me.*"

Put it together. What is he saying? The answer is the difference between Christianity and Hinduism. Reincarnation is an endless wheel, a spinning sorrow that goes nowhere. Jesus Christ is the stairway to heaven—firm, finished, forever.

"I'm supposed to believe in the devil?"

If there's one man in the gospels I think I understand, he's the one who tried to get into the boat with Jesus.

This is that Bible story that makes the hairs on your arm stand up, at first anyway. The man shared his skin with demons. He lived his nightmare among the tombs. He screamed all night, every night. He cut himself with stones. Then one day he spoke those chilling words to Jesus with a voice not his own: "My name is Legion, for we are many." I dare you to think of these words tonight as you climb the basement stairs.

These evil spirits, of all creatures, knew the "Son of the Most High" when he stood before them. They knew that who-do-you-think-you-are look on God's face, that exquisite anger when someone so evil has touched one dear to him. They knew when they weren't wanted, and they just went away. Why? Jesus told them to.

Imagine you're that man. No more chains that can't keep out the horror, or no more nights spent alone with evil. No more torturous fear that no one can touch. It's over. Because of Jesus. It's enough to make you wade out in the water and throw a knee up over the side of an old wooden fishing boat, spending not a single thought on where the boat is going. Anywhere with him is fine with you. You've never been more sane than at this point, right now, locking eyes with Jesus, begging, "Take me with you."

Jesus' answer is not no; it is "not yet." "Go home to your family and tell them how much the Lord has done for you, and how he has had mercy on you."

You see, we are talking about the devil, but that doesn't mean it's going to be about fear. It's about gratitude, the kind that puts a lump in your throat and a shine in your eyes. There's a thank you God's lips have formed in your heart, one you'll never get over as long as you're in your right mind. Only remember the difference between the One who has you now and the one who had you before.

(Please read Mark 5:1-20.)

Do you feel a chill as you imagine a séance? Does your skin crawl as you think about the pointer on that *Ouija* board that moved by itself? And if so, *why* does it crawl? Think about it. Just as humor isn't humorous if there's no grain of truth to it, what if it's the same way with horror? Consider movies like *The Exorcist* and novels by Stephen King. What is the bit of truth behind the terror?

I once sat through a long night with a young woman who was literally paralyzed with fear of the "man" that came to her every night, whispering, "Stay away from those Christians. You're mine." Unable to speak, trembling, barely able to move for the fright, she would jump and shriek as if she was being prodded and poked. I've heard similar accounts from people I know well . . . how it took four men to hold down a frightened, frightening child as he struggled for several hours. This from level-headed people who know what psychosis is, and what it isn't. Believe me, even in my Christian circles, we are not at all prone to see demons within every tortured mind. But sometimes you can't deny them. Psychologist and author Gary Collins commented, "Whereas twenty-five years ago the suggestion of demonic activity would have been immediately dismissed, many psychologists are beginning to recognize that maybe there are more things in heaven and earth than our philosophies can account for."[94]

Normally, it seems Satan is content to be dismissed as an ancient superstition. He may be better served by disbelief than by outright worship of himself. It's rather elementary that if the devil were shown to be real, Jesus would be also. By howling at me in my bed Satan could accomplish nothing other than chasing me closer to Christ. Yet even when he refrains from unmasking himself in overt supernatural displays, it's clear he's been busy. Some things can only be called evil.

Horrid fascination with the occult steadily grows. I've seen videotape of a rock star hollering, "Who wants to go to hell?" and ten thousand teenagers chanting, "We do." Some of those teens will kill themselves, not because they're desperate or scared but because they aren't scared enough. For God's sake, they're curious!

There are people who would kill God (again) if they could. What they can do is kill Christians, more in this century than in all those that have come before, more because of the faith they hold than the beliefs of any others. (You didn't know that, did you?) There are people who take pleasure in the pain they are able to cause others. The commandment of Satanism, "Do what you will is the whole of the law," has won cultural acceptability as a valid personal philosophy. The end-times prophecy "People will be lovers of themselves"[95] rings true as more and more people celebrate pride and self-preoccupation as virtues. And Christ is still the name most often taken in vain. People have learned these things from one who usually wishes to remain anonymous but whose footprints are unmistakable.

You may have a big problem with the notion of a devil. But once you realize that all the beautiful things in this world are *personal*—that there is a good and beautiful *Someone* smiling behind every good thing—it's no stretch to realize the same is true about evil. Evil is personal too. There's a dreadful *someone* behind it all, a twisted mind, an evil intention. Beneath the sounds of human wreckage—another family torn to weeping pieces, another woman undone by her own desires, another little boy destroyed by another sick man—you can almost hear the sound of someone laughing.

But let's be very clear about who the devil is, very clear about how the Scriptures consistently portray him. Don't think of the devil as the opposite of God. He's bad enough to be that, but he's not big enough. The devil is powerful but he's not a god; he is not even close. He's merely another creature. By the way, hell is his prison cell, not his home.

God made angels to watch over us that are so beautiful that people who saw them were tempted to worship them. Satan and his demons were originally holy angels as well. All angels were given the same freedom offered to Adam and Eve. God's desire was that in his creation would be found such a thing as love, for love is the highest possible good in the universe. But to offer that highest good—the freedom to love God and one another—required the possibility that they would choose *not* to exercise it. They were not to be only puppets, and their praise was not to be merely automatic noise. This choice was not a meaningless exercise with nothing at stake, not an experiment to be started over anytime it went wrong. The game would have to be played out no matter what. They would have to live and die with their decisions, just as God would. Especially God.

Satan and his kind are the angels that made that unsmiling, insanely proud choice against the Lord of heaven. That God allowed that event and all its consequences is the awful, necessary part of his beautiful plan, one that includes things not otherwise possible. Consider that deeper revelation of God crying on a cross, that deeper joy on the other side of the grave, and that deeper glory of the saints in heaven, singing the song of the redeemed in the presence of the Lamb and then bending their faces toward transparent gold.

Ever since he fell, Satan has been about taking you with him instead, possessing you, although not necessarily in the overtly terrifying way we see in the gospel accounts. He wants to keep you in the spiritual dark he authored.

"The god of this age has blinded the minds of unbelievers, so that they cannot see the light of the gospel of the glory of Christ, who is the image of God."[96]

The devil will do anything, say anything, to obscure the lovely face of Christ, to keep us blind to our soul's only treasure, and to savor the ancient human shame. In this he is tireless. He knows no mercy, and he will not stop. From all around, day in and day out, come messages meant to deceive you about God—he isn't what you need, he can't be known, he won't forgive, he isn't to be trusted, he isn't good, he isn't even real. This is satanic language from "the father of lies."[97] And the really chilling thing is that the brainwashed don't know they are brainwashed.

Saint Augustine, a Christian bishop from the early fifth century, for a time felt the devil's claim on his own soul. Although as a young man he had given himself over to sexual immorality many times over, that wasn't what brought him the fiercest terrors of conscience. Instead, it was the fact that he had once stolen some apples. While his sexual sins could be explained by his physical desire for pleasure, there was something *else* in his theft of apples. The bald fact was that he didn't really want them. What he wanted was the sheer malevolence of taking them and destroying them. Augustine saw in himself a satanic love of being bad, an unholy pleasure in despising God and rebelling against the good. It scared him to death. What about you? Is it really so unreasonable to pray the words Jesus left behind for you, "Deliver us from evil"?

Your cry has been heard. Your prayer was answered long before you had the heart to pray it. "Now the prince of this world will be driven out. But I, when I am lifted up from the earth, will draw all men to myself."⁹⁸ Jesus proclaimed this shortly before he died. Even as he hung on the cross, as Satan's defeat was being written in holy blood, the "drawing" had begun. As if a spell was being broken as the holy wind blew around that hill, a dying thief begged, "Jesus, remember me." A murderous centurion said, "Surely this man was the Son of God." Like a broken spell. As the cry "It is finished" still rings through every world there is, a noose still tightens around Satan's neck.

There's an Old Testament prophecy about the Lord that reads, "He will pursue his foes into darkness."⁹⁹ Though these words were written against the vicious nation of Assyria, I can't help but relate them also to that day when the risen Lord Jesus descended into hell to declare his victory over our merciless enemy, the devil. Similar are the chilling words God spoke to Nineveh, as captured by the original Hebrew. It literally reads, "See me . . . *against you*."¹⁰⁰

And it's my enemy, Satan, I think of as the prophecy goes on: "Everyone who hears the news about you claps his hands at your fall, for who has not felt your endless cruelty?" And I clap my hands as well.

So when a petrified girl heard the father of lies say "You're mine," I only had to read to her the Word of God.

"Fear not, for I have redeemed you; I have summoned you by name; you are mine."[101] It was nothing less than the voice of her mighty Savior-God.

"Don't cry. It's over now. I've got you. Don't be afraid."

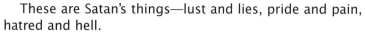

These are Satan's things—lust and lies, pride and pain, hatred and hell.

These are God's—the Word and the water, the bread and the wine, the promise of forgiveness in Jesus . . . and all those who believe.

He says to all who run to him for refuge, "I am for you."

"I live for

this world,

not a world

to come"

When Jesus looked ahead to the world's last days, this is what he saw us doing:

"Marrying and being given in marriage."

"Eating and drinking."

"Buying and selling."

"Planting and building."

This prediction, in its own way, is one of Jesus' most convicting. You ask, "What in the world is wrong with these things?" and the answer is "Nothing." These things are fine and good . . . until they crowd out the things that matter far more. And we crossed that line a long time ago.

Can you imagine a society more obsessed than us to get everything in this life just the way we like it? What are the thousands of messages about that bombard us every day but "eating and drinking," "buying and selling"? What else is there to be interested in besides who will find love where and how to get our marks high up on some wall? We sure can't think of anything. And Jesus sees it all.

When we are out there buying and selling, planting and building, we like to say we are dealing with "the real world." But that's where we're wrong. The things we can see are the temporary things. What only faith sees—forgiveness, life, peace with God—these are forever. The magnificent heart of Christ, the heavenly Father's care, and the angels he sends to watch over us day by day, these are the real world.

Are you starting to see them? Are you waking up to that world? This is a cause of celebration. Yet I must tell you that this new faith, like a young seedling reaching for the sky, can so easily be choked off. And this doesn't require overtly evil things . . . only earthly cares. You know . . .

"Marrying and being given in marriage."

"Eating and drinking."

"Buying and selling."

"Planting and building."

(Please read Luke 17:20-37.)

While Christians are always talking about some world yet to come, you say you live for this world. You say that the self-help gurus and success teachers of our day seem to be the relevant ones, because they talk about real-life problems—how to make it *here*, not in some nebulous *somewhere else*. And so we come to another point of controversy between the believers and nearly everyone else. It has to do with being "worldly."

Worldliness is shown in the way you find yourself entirely weighed down by human affairs, obsessed with the issue of making a living, wondering how it could be any other way. Worldliness has to do with your attachments. Worldliness is shown in the grief you feel over the very thought of losing your death grip on this or that thing which you have now. Beneath that grief lies the terror of one day having to leave this whole world behind and exchanging it . . . for what?

Furthermore, worldliness prefers the material and the temporary to the spiritual and the eternal, as if we were made to want no more than this world contains. As C. S. Lewis commented, "We are half-hearted creatures, fooling about with drink and sex and ambition when infinite joy is offered us, like an ignorant child who wants to go on making mud pies in a slum because he cannot imagine what is meant by the offer of a holiday at the sea. *We are far too easily pleased.*"[102]

Even more, worldliness is any controversy that exists between you and the God of the Holy Bible. You have a problem with certain things he says. Your mind calls this or that truth of God's Word harsh, intolerant, sexist, or just plain bad. You find you are far more sympathetic to the point of view you hear in the world. You would like to blame the countercultural truths of the Bible on some church's narrow interpretation, but that's an evasion. You have a problem with God. Your worldliness, like mine, is the degree to which your thinking and your very life originate from this present world and not from God.

What are we to do? Here's an analogy suggested to me by Chinese author Watchman Nee. Imagine you've worked in one company all your life. You have invested yourself entirely in that place and are counting on it to take care of you in retirement. One day you hear the news that the company is going out of business sometime very soon. It has sold you out, and not one promise your boss made is going to be kept. Out of necessity, you keep on going to work there, drawing your paycheck while it lasts. But you notice that everything has changed—how personally involved you are, how attached, how you listen to the company line. It all changed the instant you heard the business was going under. It changed because you realized that you had no future there.

This is how it must have been for old Noah between the day he first heard that the world was going to be destroyed by the flood and the day those waters arrived a hundred years later. During that time, he lived in the same world he had lived before, yet everything was different for him. In his mind he saw the shop where he bartered for saws and hammers, the town square where the desperately important issues of the day were debated (and where he was no doubt laughed at), the schools where the arts and skills were taught—he saw everything, *under water.* To say the least, this anticipation of the destruction that was coming clarified things for Noah.

The point is that you don't so much exhaust yourself in a bitter, sweaty battle with worldliness as you open merely your eyes to a simple truth. Worldliness loses its grip the minute you hear the truth for the first time—and anytime you remember it—the truth about the kind of judgment that will fall on this world and everything in it. *You have no future here.*

Ah, but perhaps one day Noah looked up at his son Shem spreading pitch on the gopher wood of the ark, and there he saw something different. *"This I take with me."*

Of all the things for Noah to see in the world, when he looked at his wife and children, it was different. *"These I get to keep."* He could see his family lifted up by the water, salvaged out of that condemned world, and set down in another. By enough water to cover the whole earth and by the wood of ten thousand trees, they were going to be saved. Noah had to be a man who was clear about his attachments—what he would leave behind and what he could take with him—clear about whom he listened to and whose promises would be kept. In mere recognition of the facts, Noah was not a worldly man.

Well, the same message (You have no future here) has come down to us. There is a future for us, but it's not here in this world. I would ask you to read the entire gospel of John. Meditate on the word *world* that confronts you 78 times in just 16 chapters. By *world* Jesus means the entire human race lined up in rebellion against its own Creator, the great mass of humanity gone out of its mind. The world is the entire earthbound system of human thinking and human institutions that have no place for Christ. And so, the world comes to mean everything that will no longer be here after the judgment comes.

As you read the gospel of John, you'll read of the Son of God acting as a light shining into the world. The world did not acknowledge him or want to. The world hated him, because he was not of this world. The world stared with incredulity at the One who taught that "life does not consist in the abundance of possessions" and to "love your neighbor as yourself."

"You're not from around here, are you?" was the look on their faces; an eternity laid between their points of view. Always he answered their look with remarkable otherworldly things: "[I didn't come] to condemn the world, but to save the world."[103] On the day he died, the world received its notice: "Now is the time for judgment on this world."[104]

There is a future for you. But it's not here. Not anymore.

This is what it means to be saved. It is to look around and to know that everything you see will be destroyed sometime very soon. Everything . . . but you. For by faith you are snatched up and held already in the hands of God. By faith you are connected to Christ and the life he already lived for you and the death that's already been died. By the waters of Holy Baptism you are inseparably bonded to Christ, the One risen from the dead. You are lifted Noah-like by water, saved by wood, and you arrive in the kingdom of God dripping wet. For your part, you "seek first his kingdom," and your God takes care of everything else. He cares for you. And so to make it through this world and to leave in your wake a life that has been well lived, you've learned to want something else. *"I want to know Christ."*

The world may admire the charity Christians perform, but when we hold out the thing itself, the Christ, the world only hates us as it first hated him. "You're not from around here," it says, and we're not. We are "in the world, but not of the world." The essential question is not about how much good we do but about where we're from. There is no working our way to heaven. The essential question asks about where we are from, this faith, and this new life.

"Everyone who believes that Jesus is the Christ is born of God."[105]

As I write, I remember my time doing home mission work, planting and building a church in Rockford, Illinois. I can still see a hundred Christians giving their best to construct a sanctuary. What they are about has little to do with making this world a better place. They are about declaring the truth about Jesus. The sacred space they create, at great personal cost, seems about as practical as a boat built a thousand miles from the sea.

From this place they share Jesus, like a hand held open to the cosmos. "You have no future here. Oh, save yourselves from this entangling world. Come away with us."

We believers sat in a circle, with Bibles lying open on our laps. The kingdom of God was made so vivid, so real, that the world receded before the Word. Together we reached the upper room, high above the level of the street. All we saw was Jesus—the sacrifice broke our hearts, but he is alive. Our minds were taken up with the forgiveness we celebrate and the glory for which we wait. We set aside worldly concerns. We washed one another's feet. We washed the world away.

There's nothing wrong with the stuff we have or the matters that busy us—mutual funds, answering machines, grocery lists—except for the film that begins to cover our eyes the instant the Word is gone from our hearts.

Jesus, leave us not alone. Send your Holy Spirit. Let us surrender every argument our minds make against your Word. Let us see the nothingness of the possessions stacking up all around us. Let us see you, and let these words escape our souls: "Earth has nothing I desire besides you."[106]

Let me see my little girl smearing grape jelly all over the wall.

This I get to keep.

"I'll be rejected by family and friends"

Do you realize there is a time in the gospels when we can hear Jesus' own family say, "He is out of his mind"? On one occasion it's enough for his siblings to encourage their big brother Jesus to go as far away as possible. Another time they actually try to "take charge of him." What Jesus has to say on such an occasion that involves his immediate family is important for you to hear if you face rejection by family or friends for his sake.

It's about having a new family, a spiritual one.

He is surrounded on all sides by a crowd when the message reaches him, "Your mother and brothers are outside looking for you." The interruption stops him short. It causes him to look again at the people all around, his quiet, captive audience. They aren't his blood relatives, at least not in the way we usually mean. They are, however, the ones who are sitting and listening. These are the people with spirits turned toward him, who reflect in their faces whatever he shows them in his. He has something for them. You might even say that he puts himself up for adoption. With a magnanimous, sweeping gesture, he cries out, *"Here are my mother and my brothers!"*

Never mind if it seems harsh to his immediate family. It doesn't mean he has given up on them. Far from it. It does mean that he has a gift for anyone who has ever lost someone— a brother, a sister, a parent—for his sake.

"Whoever does God's will is *my* brother and sister and mother."

(Please read Luke 4:14-30 and Mark 3:20-35.)

It's not something I've had to go through, so I don't speak lightly about it, but I've seen it happen to other people. They've found something in Jesus crucified that answers all the really big questions in life. The reality of Christ brings a fullness and light they had not imagined, and they positively have to tell people about him. Who but their family and friends? When they do, however, they are met by a certain coldness in familiar faces that wasn't there before. The closer to Christ they become, the more distant their loved ones become. And it hurts.

If this is your experience already, my first encouragement is for you to try to understand the people whose rejection you are feeling. I remember well the joy felt by a young Mormon woman who left that intensely legalistic life for a life of grace in Jesus. It became clear that beneath the rage of her parents was the open wound of betrayal. It felt to them as though she was ungratefully tossing aside every- thing they had ever tried to give her. Your parents too may be feeling the sting of failure as you walk away from their worldview—whatever it happens to be—and as you set aside whatever legacy they were trying to give you, such as it was. But even now there is an honor you can pay your mom and dad. They gave you all they had, and your heartfelt thank- you for whatever that "all" was may need to be said now more than ever.

What is just as likely is that your family and perhaps your friends even more are bracing themselves for your transformation. Their radar is tuned in for hypocrisy. They are preparing themselves for the new and holier you and for awkward moments that will leave you feeling superior and them feeling condemned. Though your new self is actually far more attractive than the old one, characterized as it is by gentle humility and grateful joy, and whereas condemning is the farthest thing from your Christian mind, it is true enough that you aren't quite the person they previously knew. I remember very well a man who used to play keyboard in a rock band, but once a Christian he found he couldn't do it anymore. He didn't have the heart for it. Now he speaks up to his friends against his former lifestyle. Sadly, he doesn't know whether he'll ever change them; it has to be enough for him to know that *they* have not changed *him*. Ah, but the look on his face when I brought up the matter of using his gift in the worship of Christ! He's clearly *not* the same person anymore, and the guys *don't* come around like they used to. But what's to be said?

What's to be said is this: "Your Jesus can repay from his own fullness all he takes away."[107] Author Larry Crabb once made a statement that should have been obvious: "There's more to life than solving problems and making pain end." We make this our all-consuming passion, to finally get our little lives just so, as if that is the obvious point of living. The gift in heartache is the energy it provides as you turn with your whole being *toward Christ. He* is the point. He is the *more* in "there's more to life" than merely feeling better. The very good thing about the ache you now feel is the opportunity it gives you to find him and know him in a still deeper way. God is surely working when this emptiness has you thumbing through the Scriptures, hungry for a Word from him. Far from dismissing the pain of the loss you feel, I encourage you to fully feel its weight and to not forget it.

In this you feel your thirst, like a deer panting for water. Such is your desire for the One who loves you when mere human love runs out. All this my Lord can bless.

Next, I direct you toward your spiritual family in Christ, all your smiling new brothers and sisters. I don't do so to give you some sort of compensation or to dismiss how badly you feel. The reality of your spiritual family in Christ is a beautiful truth all the same. There are people in this world who come from and are traveling toward the same place as you. They are connected to you in the deepest place, where grace is known. They understand who you are and why you do what you do. The spiritual bond is the real one, after all. Biology is only biology. These will be your people forever.

Although in some quiet moment you may need to make the deliberate sacrifice—"Jesus, I'm willing to lose whatever is necessary for me to lose"—I am not suggesting you willingly leave people behind.

There's the moment in Matthew's gospel, his firsthand account about the life of Jesus, when his writing suddenly becomes autobiographical. He recounts the day Jesus found him in his tax collector's booth. Jesus leaned in. Strong carpenter hands gripped the corners of Matthew's table. Just two words, "Follow me," make me wonder what kind of Man this was, with what kind of presence and power. Matthew actually got up and walked away from the job, the table, the money. He left it all to fall in behind the Christ.

He left everything, that is, except his friends.

You see, the next thing Matthew did was throw a party to which he invited both his old *and* his new friends. Together in one place were the other tax collectors Matthew ran around with and also the disciples and their Lord. He didn't keep these circles of friends carefully apart. He shoved the followers of Christ and the non-followers all together into one decidedly uncomfortable mix—a beautiful, risky gesture to accomplish—well, who knows?

What does it take to be in a position to influence your family and friends with the love of Christ? You'll need to grow very strong through faithful, unhurried time with Jesus in his Word. You'll want to prepare just a bit for the way you might put your faith into words when God provides the opportunity. Someday that moment will come.

While you wait for it, what you never need to do is pretend to be something you're not or act as if you're further along in your growth than you really are. For the people who don't really know what it means to be a Christian but are pretty sure it means having to be perfect (and perfectly happy), simple honesty can go a long, long way.

Such honesty confesses: "My sin is ever with me, and I am often ashamed, but I always know I'm forgiven. Sometimes I'm very sad, I won't kid you, but I have a stubborn joy of knowing heaven is really already mine . . . and that I'm never going to die."

The last thing I want you to see is how important you have become if you should be the one person in your circle of family and friends whose eyes are opened to Jesus. I'm stirred by the answer one old man gave when his friends asked whether his life was happy. "No, not always," he replied. So they asked him how he *would* describe his life if it wasn't always happy.

"Necessary."

That's *your* life. Necessary. There's a reason for you. No other life is interchangeable with yours. Who else will love the people around you, *your* people, as Christ loves them? Whom else has God placed in the position you are in "for such a time as this"? In your circle of family and friends, even if all the rest are spiritually dead and tragically so, at least one has been made alive. It's you.

May you have the grace someday to sit them down, look them in the eyes, take a deep breath, and say something like what James Dobson said to his teenage son after the death of a friend. To paraphrase: "I'll always care about the things you do and the things that happen to you in this world. But you need to know one thing. Nothing in life matters more to me than having you with me forever in heaven. And if I know anything at all, I know that the only way is Jesus Christ. I'm tearing my heart open for you now, because this is certain: someday I'll be looking for your face in heaven. I'll be searching that great city Jerusalem for you. And whatever else you ever do, I beg you, take another look at Jesus. You see I love you. And I want you to *be there*."

My family, my friends, all my dear ones . . . *be there!*

And so, after Jesus has risen from the dead and has ascended into heaven, we're taken to an upper room where the believers have gathered. The disciples of Christ are praying. The Eleven are all there, of course, along with the women and Mary, his mother.[108] But the ones that make me smile right now?

The little brothers of Jesus.

"Why the endless quibbling over teachings?"

They say life is a teacher, and it may be so.

But we are prone to learn all the wrong things.

I once read about a series of rather heartless experiments performed on a poor, unsuspecting mouse. The mouse's cage held everything a mouse knows how to enjoy—mouse food, mouse water, mouse delights, mouse pastimes. When an electric shock was administered to the metal cage floor just once, the creature ran out the door of his cage one time, two times . . . many times. So what did the mouse learn from its life? From a single experience of pain, it learned to run away from everything it needed.

Next they put the mouse back in the cage and held the door closed just long enough for the mouse to stop pushing on it. After that the mouse could have left its cage at any time, but from a single frustration, it learned that there was nothing it could do. It felt it was useless to try.

Lastly, more electric shocks were administered, one after another. The hapless mouse just lay there pathetically and took it. Experience in the cage had taught the mouse well. There it learned futility and hopeless resignation.

They say life is a teacher. What have you learned?

Did you let someone get close to you and end up hurt and in pain? Did you learn to make sure it would never happen again? Did things not work out the way you hoped, no matter how hard you worked at them? Did you learn not to try? Did you ever lie in your bed as the sun warmed another morning and remember what you were supposed to do with the day but for the life of you not remember why you were to do it?

What have you been learning from life? Are you ready to unlearn it? Is it time for a new teacher? Think of the invitation of the One who lived so beautifully and died so gracefully and overcame death so completely: "Learn *from me.*" Be awakened to how badly you need to learn from him. Left to ourselves we know precious little, but there stands Jesus.

"Come and learn from me."

He was talking to the worn-out ones on the verge of giving up. He was promising rest, sweet rest, to answer the bone-tiredness of their souls. I look into the sayings of mere men—Buddha, Confucius, Gandhi, Muhammad—and no one looks back. While the words of the would-be guides lie exhausted on the page, the weary millions are still plumbing the depths of Christ and are still being made new, still being set free.

This is the testimony of the countless thousands of books and poems, works of art and songs Jesus inspires to this very day. He is the one Teacher of old who is teaching still.

(Please read Matthew 11:25-30.)

Some people have an aversion to the church's doctrinal formulas *about* God, as if they were a poor substitute for an actual encounter *with* God—"I'd rather experience an ocean than study a map of one." It's C. S. Lewis who pointed out that uncharted oceans are perilous places and that having a reliable map makes the difference between life and death. To know God at all is to know that there is unspeakable danger in his untamed holiness for sinners like us. What, then, is sound theology but a faithful charting of the one safe channel into the loving heart of God?

"No one comes to the Father except through me,"[109] said Jesus.

Some people can only shake their heads at such a church that once split into an East and a West over a single word in the Nicene Creed. Wasn't unity more important than a mere syllable or two of compromise? Why couldn't the church budge just an inch one way or the other? G. K. Chesterton observed that when one is engaged in a delicate balancing act, an inch is everything. Indeed, millions plunge into human pride on the one hand and human despair on the other, all for want of the steadying words of Christ.

"I am the way."[110]

Others find church teachings and the squabbles about them distasteful because they find the people doing the squabbling distasteful. Perhaps these others were at the receiving end of endless dogmatic assertions in an environment that excluded honest questioning. Such dissenters are right to reject the pride they see at work in combative, graceless teachers. A wonderful analogy about church doctrines comes from the book *Fearfully and Wonderfully Made* by Paul Brand and Philip Yancey. Church teachings are like the bones in the human body. Though they are alive, they are also hard and inflexible, refusing to change their shape— bones present the very qualities that separate human beings from slithering slugs. Bones allow us to walk and run, jump and dance. They allow eagles to soar.

At the same time, we aren't crustaceans either, coldly wearing our bones on the outside. Our bones are wrapped in the warmth of our human skin so that our soft, touchable flesh is the first thing people encounter. It must be this way for the church and its teachings. The model is that people should first see our love and be treated to an experience of grace at our hands and from our lips in order to know just whose disciples we are. The teachings we have from Christ and our refusals to compromise or tamper with them are to be wrapped in the warmth and human-kindness that come from him as well. *Speak "the truth in love."*[111] This is his command.

There are two points I am making. One, there is a humble and loving way of presenting church teachings, and two, the issues being presented matter more than one can say. The issues surrounding God and our relationship to him are life and death ones, spiritually speaking. You must not insist that we who care about such things should agree to disagree just as you would not ask physicians to politely compromise when they disagree about the best way to keep a patient alive. Say what you want about doctrinal disputes, but don't merely disengage, dismissing them as mere quibbling about nothing. What is more foundational to life and the way we live it than what our souls say about God? Where you direct the terrified conscience is the difference between hope and despair. What you say to poor sinners needing peace is a matter of life and death. Christ crucified is our hope. There is no other. He is reality, not abstraction.

Thus Christ stands in sharpest contrast to that shadow, the postmodern god about whom no dogmas are believed . . . who produces no fear in which wisdom can begin . . . who creates no love in which wisdom can be complete . . . for whose sake no one denies anything, risks anything, ventures anything . . . and neither does this god ask. The Bible declares that one of the judgments people receive for believing such false ideas about God is the confusion itself.[112] Lies about God only put the shame back into life and the fear back into death and lead the lost further and further away.

Before you reject all doctrinal distinctions out of hand as if they are trivial, consider the most important church doctrine of all, the foundation upon which "the church either stands or falls." If you do know the terrors of conscience, if you know something of guilt like steel wool always scrubbing at the heart, if you've sinned enough to *give up already* on your own goodness . . . it's about time. You are prepared to understand the magnificent truth we call *objective justification*. This term answers the question, Just what did Jesus Christ accomplish on his cross? God has declared the whole world innocent for Jesus' sake. It is a matter of Christian dogma that salvation is a finished fact for every person and that God extends this gift freely to everyone, no matter who you are or what you've done. You only believe. Trust God that in Christ he has already forgiven the sins of every human being. He is the *not* in your not guilty verdict.

He loves you. He always has. He accepts you. *You!*

This is one of those church doctrines that some people find so distasteful, the one that will just happen to save you in every way a person can be saved if you have ears to hear. When you believe it, a light pierces your private darkness. This light shines everywhere and on everything, illuminating death and the way it is met and giving clear definition to life and what it is for after all. We mine the very heart of God. The preeminent characteristics of sound theology are that it takes God's Word seriously in every thing that it says, that it gives all glory to Christ in every aspect of life and salvation, and that it gives maximum comfort to the soul that has once seen its desperate spiritual condition!

Perhaps you can see why we don't pick and choose among a menu of Bible teachings—"This one I like. . . . This one not so much." Perhaps you believe that "Jesus loves me" and want to say that this is all that really matters. The truth is that virtually any false teaching, for example, "Salvation is by human choice," if it is carried out to its logical conclusion, will attack your assurance of God's grace. Even "Jesus loves me" can be lost in the end. Notice, please, that objective justification and all other points of Christian teaching hang together as a beautiful, organic unity. They form an unspoiled portrait of Christ, which can't be improved by any human contribution, only obscured by it.

Those still outside of Christ may prefer a formless, shapeless "church" that says and stands for nothing, that is, no church at all. Just don't expect me to agree. I've spent too many hours in dusty old books of pristine biblical theology, teachings untouched by man. Orthodox Christian doctrine is really nothing more than a systematic repetition of the Bible's clearest verses. I far too consistently find that there is life, real life, to be found in Christian dogma when it is handled with the highest possible precision. I review every beautiful thing we are trying to say when we say "grace alone" and "faith alone." I remember the delicate mystery of the person of Christ. I see, as if for the first time, what grace *is*.

And my soul delights in God.
My spirit soars like an eagle *to him*.

What you must not argue is that endless questions are better than God's final answers. Don't try arguing that darkness is better than light with one who has seen that light. Christian doctrine is not designed for your moral improvement or for endless human debate. The body of Christian *teaching*, handled with exquisite attention to detail, will always lead you back to *the Teacher*. It is designed to make you alive to God and to lead you back to the Truth in human skin.

You are not expected to become some sort of walking encyclopedia of biblical information. You may never win at *Bible Trivia*. Though it is a good thing, a very good thing, whenever you hide God's Word in your heart, it's just not about volume.

The learning I desire for you is of a different kind. May you yearn to see clean to the bottom of . . . to exhaust the meaning behind . . . to catch a glimpse of everything held waiting within . . . just two words off the lips of Christ.

"Lord, teach us to pray," pleaded his disciples.

And what Jesus said in reply! Ah, you, dear Jesus!

When you pray to the Holiness, Almighty Creator, Judge of the world, Life of all life, pray this way. Say . . .

"Our Father . . ."

"Why is there so much pain in the world?"

One of the "untouchables" of the ancient world is on his knees in front of Jesus. Then he's face down in the dirt. The man has leprosy, a disease that not only disfigures the sufferer but perhaps even worse, it isolates him from his community and even his own family and friends.

You can only wonder how long this broken man has watched his children grow up from afar or how long he's lumbered through life shouting "Unclean!" to keep every other soul at a safe distance. How long has it been since he has known the feel of another person's skin against his own? No wonder he is on his knees, then flat on his face before the Lord. It's a good place to be.

You can almost hear the gasp of the crowd at what Jesus does in response. It wouldn't seem worth mentioning if you didn't understand the horrific effects of leprosy, the terror of the disease, and the dreadful withdrawal of human contact. But all three gospels that carry this scene detail the spontaneous reaching of Jesus' hand.

He touched the leper.

Why? The gospels only answer that Jesus was "filled with compassion."

Where is God when it hurts? Hurting right along with us. And in the Word of kindness and peace, crossing the gap from living God to dying sinner, is where God is found.

(Please read Mark 1:40-45.)

The disease of leprosy is an interesting place to begin a chapter about the problem of pain. (I'm indebted to Philip Yancey's example in his thoughtful treatment on suffering, *Where Is God When It Hurts?*) Though the term *leprosy* has been used to describe a variety of skin diseases, in its most horrifying form, leprosy is associated with gross physical disfigurements—the loss of fingers, toes, eyes, noses, and so on. Dr. Paul Brand is the man who discovered that this type of leprosy doesn't actually destroy human tissue at all. All it does is remove the sensation of pain. He observed the damage leprosy patients do *to themselves* because they lack the warning signals that a healthy pain network in the human body provides. They live in a "painless hell." A boy reaches into a fire for a potato or turns a stuck key in a lock so hard his hands bleed. A man keeps walking on a broken foot or is unaware of dangerous infections in his body. A woman doesn't blink out the irritations in her eye, and so it goes. One can actually come to praise the living God for pain, that is, for the marvelous design of our bodies in which physical pain alerts us to problems, forcing us to pay attention and take care of them. Pain helps keep us healthy and alive.

Yet who can argue with the fact that pain sometimes rages out of control in our world, far beyond the boundaries of its healthy, biological function? When it does and when we have to watch helplessly, we can hardly avoid the question: How can a God of infinite love and effortless power fail to act?

Where to begin? Yancey observed, "The opposite of disappointment with God is disappointment *without* God." Suffering remains a problem no matter what philosophy you hold. In fact, Ravi Zecharias suggests answering the question, "Where is God when it hurts?" with, "Where is *atheism* when it hurts?" Atheism is that which steals away all hope and every worthwhile reason to endure. Without God, we would not only have to live with pain but with something far worse, *meaningless* pain. Denying God because of pain doesn't make pain go away. All that would go away then is the hope that pain can have a purpose, that it can lead to powerful good, that it's never for nothing, that it can be redeemed in the end.

It is the Christian faith that properly names the cause of pain. I've already written to you that the ultimate cause of the world's misery is human sin. I'm not suggesting each particular pain can be traced to a particular sin. (Although I would submit that a huge portion of the world's suffering—physical tortures and relational torments—is directly caused by people. And let no one say in such circumstances, "It was God's will." His will and his plan is to bring good from every evil for those who know him and trust him.) As for the cause of pain, what I am saying is that just as horrifying as the symptom is, namely pain, so dreadful is its first cause. Sin is that great and willful abandonment of God by the human race.

In fact, consider the premise that sin is something far *worse* than pain. Anyone who has been to the dentist knows that pain, on the one hand, can have good purposes. Pain can so often bring people around the ultimate matters of faith. Pain is, in the words of C. S. Lewis, "God's megaphone to rouse a deaf world." Suffering wins our attention in a way and to a depth nothing else ever does, humbling us enough to cry out to him. Sin, on the other hand, is our determination to shut him out, to somehow make life make sense *apart* from him. Do you see the difference? Pain hurts; sin is death. Pain makes us cry for a while. Sin would have made us cry forever, had God not done something about it.

But cry for a while we do. I purposely write this chapter while the people I visited with last night are fresh in my mind. They are no spectators on the sidelines of suffering. Their daughter was 13 years old when she died. Before she died, she had suffered. Horribly. Let's call her Katie. She's been gone for a while now, but it still hurts her family members like it happened yesterday. I keep them in mind so that I remember what pain is and what it is like, not wishing to venture answers that are easier than the ones God gives. Perhaps a safe place to start is to tell you what Katie would if she were here. She would tell you (she did tell her family and friends) that life in this world is only an introduction to another life, one that is better by far for those who follow Jesus. Knowing this makes all the difference.

If it were not true, if this world were the whole show, I suppose we could say that God ought to make things here as pleasant as possible. (But how? I still wonder. I mean, if God were to remove *every* cause of pain in this world, where would that leave us? Truly *"he does not treat us as our sins deserve."*[113]) However, if this life is a brief shadow of a more solid world to come, a temporary prelude to a sweeter song that goes on and on, what then? Then suffering would be necessary in ways we could not be expected to fully see; it could have purposes that justify it being allowed to continue on and do its work, especially if those purposes are eternally good and cannot be achieved in any other way. Now what is noticeable right away is that trust would be central to this arrangement. We would have to have a reason to rely on those purposes, that goodness, that future.

Have I mentioned Jesus? Whatever is really wrong with this world—something we can only see in part—God's answer for it goes beyond mere easy explanations. He answers with himself, not a bunch of words or a tightly woven argument that wouldn't help us anyway. He answers with the ripping and writhing of Calvary that perfectly conforms to the misery of the world, no less awful, no less real. God's answer to pain is *God himself racked with pain*—God crying with us, God suffering with us, God dying in no one's arms.

The most remarkable act of God is that occasion when he did not act at all . . . when men swung and laughed, cursed and struck and pounded. Visit again the sacred occasion through the vivid detail of the Scriptures: "Before your very eyes Jesus Christ was clearly portrayed as crucified."[114] When you hear the gentle command of God's Spirit in the Word— "Take this. This is for you."—you do as told. This faith means that God has showed up; God has acted; God has done something mighty . . . in you.

"There is so much pain in the world" we like to say, even though the pain of all people in the world does not really accumulate, even though it is not actually experienced by any single person. No, I take that back. There is one, and only one, who *carried all our sorrows*. It is he, Jesus, who keeps me believing in the infinite goodness, power, and love of God and who tells me it makes sense to trust him no matter the "What-I-would-do-if-I-were-God" arguments this world imagines it has the right to make. These are my bottom lines: If I would believe this life is all there is and would not know of the crucifixion of God's only Son, if I would not have my own small glimpse of the surpassing joy of Christ, I would not venture any answer to the problem of pain. But God's Son *is* a gift great enough to compel me to wait on him, and God's eternal heaven *is* a place grand enough to redeem the temporary pain of those who trust him. "Our present sufferings are not worth comparing with the glory that will be revealed in us."[115]

"Not worth comparing"? Not even belonging on the same scale? Yes, a thing can be both huge and yet nothing compared to something else. Can we even imagine a joy that could dwarf into insignificance such suffering as we've seen? Though we cannot, everything will change when the story ends and we are standing there. The apostle Paul's hope-filled metaphor will bare itself fully to us: if this world groans, it groans not as a man being tortured, waiting for an end, but as a woman in childbirth, waiting for her child. Through Christ, the world's pain is that sort that can be overwhelming and intense . . . and all in a moment forgotten. For the joy is there. That's what I understand by faith about suffering. And perhaps we understand that more than this, it is neither helpful nor possible for us to know. So let us "submit to the Father of our spirits and live."[116]

Very recently I spoke with a young Christian woman who endured a recurring depression and who fearfully, desperately wanted to know how to keep it from happening again. I asked her to do a very simple thing. The next time she could feel the darkness swinging round for her again, I told her she should remember Jesus. I said to her, "What if he were sitting next to you in this chair right here and he looked into your eyes with those liquid eyes of his, the ones that have seen every sad thing in the world, and said: "Sweetheart, would you do this *for me?* Are you willing?"

And she cried even as she gave me the clearest, loveliest smile. "I never thought of that," she whispered. And she was willing. God didn't say, "Figure me out," but, "Follow me." I am reminded of how many times and in how many ways it is the way a person *responds* to suffering that determines the outcome, whether bad or good. One person spreads the pain around; another, like Katie, quite simply shines.

This is the verse we test and test again and never find wanting: "In all things God works for the good of those who love him."[117] For to *love* God, to desire *him*, to want *him*, is to find that all of life conspires for this, your highest good. Even pain works this benediction—especially pain. It turns you to him.

As for me, I have much to learn. But here's what I try to do, in my own weak way, about my own small pain. It's a path I follow in my mind, suggested to me by the writings of the late Henri Nouwen. I find that I can take every particular pain I feel—loneliness, or a headache, or desperate inadequacy—and follow it back to *the pain,* that of this whole world. I merely taste my tiny share of that inexpressible misery of this human race—so much pain and shame and fear. Should I not have my small cup to drink? In my particular pain, I am one clod of dirt connected to the vast human continent and to the great, terrible truth of the fallenness of this place. From there I follow the pain toward the man "familiar with suffering."[118]

Surely he carried all our sorrows! All the pain of the entire world made its way into the soul of Christ. Now each particular pain is inviting us closer to him, to walk softly into his compassion for this pain-wracked world. We learn not to cry for ourselves alone, we who know our place in the love of God, who are going to be in the joy of God forever. Blessed are we who mourn for the way we are comforted. But what about the others? Tears for ourselves can become something else—cry for this world along with him.

In these thoughts you are being drawn deeper into the magnificent heart of Christ.

A very good place to be.

Elie Wiesel, as a young and bitter survivor of the atrocities of a Nazi concentration camp, first poured out his story in horrifying and painful detail to a Christian man he happened to meet.

What say you? Should the man have answered with a simplistic back-pocket reply or a fine-sounding, well-rehearsed argument? Or did the situation cry for something else, the sort of thing we learn from Christ?

Without thinking twice, without saying a word, the "little Christ" embraced the thin and broken Jewish man . . . and wept.

"Who can really say what death *means?"*

The town of Nain rested on the side of a hill. It was surrounded by a wall that had one gate. As Jesus led his crowd of followers up the path toward the city, a funeral procession was leaving town by the same narrow road. Picture two human parades silently slipping past each other. The one with the coffin was led by a widow grieving for her only son. If you've seen grief, you'll have no trouble imagining her. If you've seen death, you can picture her son. Leading the other parade was the Author of life.

When Jesus saw the widow, "his heart went out to her." It was not her first sorrowing walk down this hill. Not her first funeral. As he watched her pass, there was a release of his Spirit at that broken place, a promise of things to come. "Don't cry," he said.

Only it wasn't the same weak sentence I say when I can't think of anything else. When this One orders an end to tears, there is something behind the command to stop a heart, or to start one. There's a look on his face that would be outrageous on any other: "I can fix this."

But his next words aren't to the woman. Having stopped the procession with a forbidden touch on the coffin, he spoke to the young man lying dead. We could each stand such a pause in our long walks toward the grave just to hear the next eight words of Jesus.

These words sparkle with infinite possibilities here under the shadow of death. One sentence from Christ makes a joke out of all the worldly "possibility thinkers" who imagine their minds soaring unfettered when they prattle on about seven figure salaries and repeat their mantra: "If you can see it, you can be it." They still think deep inside the suffocating box when they dream of things they'll enjoy for a second or two in this life before they "rage, rage against the dying of the light."[119] But you, step outside, and just try to exhaust the possibilities stored within these eight words. Unhinge your mind. What if there is One who can speak this way to a boy lying dead?

"Young man, I say to you, get up!"

Don't miss the word *I*. By whose authority does Jesus dismiss death? His own. The young man got up, and Jesus "gave him back to his mother." And all who saw it spoke better than they knew: "God has come to help his people."

For his words slipped beneath the long shadow of death and began to peel it back.

(Please read Luke 7:11-16.)

People have numerous reasons for believing in life after death. For many their reason is a feeling. Some sense intuitively that the scientific law on the indestructibility of matter and energy—the way these can't ever really be destroyed—applies also to their own consciousness. Some see the principle of life coming out of death written across nature itself—the exploding life of spring that always follows the apparent death of winter. They ponder every seed that falls to the ground and "dies" to release a new kind of life.

Scientific laws and seeds are not proof of anything. However, the intuition itself *is* proof of something, especially because of the fact that most people admit to it. Our unshakeable sense that life somehow goes on recalls the ancient Scripture: God has *"set eternity in the hearts of men."*[120] C. S. Lewis commented that for hunger there is such a thing as food, for thirst there is such a thing as water, for human sexuality there is such a thing as, you know . . . and when we find in ourselves a longing that nothing in this world satisfies, it is another sign that there is more than what we see now. There is something more, something after.

So C. S. Lewis wrote about a dear friend who had died: "Nothing could have changed my idea of death more than Johnson did simply by dying. When the idea of Johnson and the idea of death met in my mind, *it was the idea of death that had changed.*" The complete annihilation of his friend's existence was inconceivable. He could not get his mind wrapped around it. More of this intuition of the afterlife can be seen in the strange human fear of both ghosts and corpses. When any living thing is cut in two, we find both pieces appalling. This is death—the unnatural severing of body and spirit. The body decays, but what happens to the soul? People are dying to find out.

Now, I can understand how people respond to the reality of death. I realize it's simply because people are hurting when someone has died that they feel an impulse to deny God because of it. Mourning is the price we pay for the privilege of having loved another human being. We pay dearly, and anger is one of the things we're likely to experience along the way. If you are mourning someone now, if you feel lost and without hope, I hold out the assurance that you won't always feel this way. Whether the 60 years you had your husband or the 7 years you had that little boy, you will realize one day that you wouldn't trade those years for anything in the world and that they came from a good God.

This whisper of gratitude blinks small but alive at the end of your tunnel of grief.

Most of all, I pray it enters your mind that if you deny God because of death, you haven't done anything about death at all. All you've banished is every possible hope of an *answer* for death, every possible hope that you might still see your dear ones again. Still, I've learned to listen, just listen, when grieving people need to vent the anguish in their hearts. They're just in pain, that's all.

But the one response to death that I can't at all understand is the shrug of the shoulders as if, "Oh well, no one can really know what dying is all about, and in the end it doesn't matter." Much truer it is to say that the riddle of death is the only question that does matter. If we don't know what death means, if it remains the nasty undefined variable at the end of our equation, then life itself is without solution.[121] Whatever else your life may hold in pleasures or sorrows, if you don't know what death means waiting inevitably in the end, you can't know what any of it means.

And nothing sounds less true than the world's hypocritical indifference to death—one minute outraged about a senseless murder, the next saying death is as natural as being born. Does anyone really believe that? The hopeless grief of the atheist at the funeral of a friend is surely the worst kind there is, but those are honest tears. Death is natural? We're okay with it? Surely it resounds in a far deeper place to watch Jesus cry at the tomb of his friend, as if before a tragedy. A tragedy! And he sees it better than we.

Death is an unwelcome intrusion into a world that wasn't prepared for it, the enemy coming to take away every single thing you could ever have. More than that, death is a great and terrible disgrace. This is how one man put it, "I'm not so much afraid of my death as ashamed of it." The hand that types these words will be a skeleton one day. And do you dare to ask why? It's unavoidable biblical truth that death is a consequence of sin. If you've ever seen human death, not all dressed up in a funeral parlor but as it actually is, then you've witnessed one thing that matches the ugliness of human guilt and have heard the sharpest possible teaching of God's law.

So soon after the opening pages of the Bible record the entrance of human sin into the world, we encounter in the ancient Hebrew text the word *vayamoth.* We read it again and again and again. It tolls like a bell throughout the ancient genealogy, after each man's name for generation upon generation: *". . . vayamoth . . . vayamoth . . . vayamoth . . ."*
". . . and he died . . . and he died . . . and he died . . ."
These are "the wages of sin."[122] The sad truth is that we are dying already as we live. Walter Wangerin observed that when a bucket is being poured out, the last drop does not *empty* the bucket; it is simply the last step in a process that went on the entire time. While we live, our lives are already running away. Our bodies are returning to dust. But again, what of our souls?

This is the ultimate fear, the one that holds all people captive for all their lives, that makes them waste their lives running from the inevitable, the one that they must push to the back of the closet, that surfaces in nightmares and debilitating phobias, silly euphemisms, neurotic denials, and contradictory philosophies—the fear of death and whatever it brings.

And yet the ugliest scene in the entire world and in all recorded history is that of nails being driven through the palms of Christ as he faced all our consequences. This was the cost of the way he chose to love us—the dead body of God was planted deep in our human soil. Like a seed . . . a stubborn, unstoppable, inevitable seed.

And the most beautiful scene etched in human history is *Jesus Christ alive.* Please don't deny it too quickly. It is all we really have. To paraphrase C. S. Lewis: "Nothing has changed my view of death more than Jesus did simply by dying. When he and death met, *it was death that was changed.*" And the living Savior, through the Word he has left us, is the one who has a right to speak when your heart wants to know what death means, for your dear one, for you. Let the agnostic stare blankly at his feet, having nothing whatsoever to say. It is Christ who fulfilled the marvelous prophecy Isaiah once made over the very Jerusalem—"on this mountain"—where Christ appeared alive from the dead: "On this mountain he will destroy the shroud that enfolds all peoples, the sheet that covers all nations; he will swallow up death forever. The Sovereign LORD will wipe away the tears from all faces; he will remove the disgrace of his people from all the earth."[123]

The resurrection of Jesus Christ justifies the human longing for life to go on and more than completely satisfies it. In Jesus the general principle that dead people stay dead now has an asterisk beside it, one outrageous footnote. The "firstfruits"[124] appeared on the human tree, with the promise of more "fruit" to follow. It is Christ who walked through death and emerged alive and smiling on the other side, who pushed open a door closed for centuries and left it open behind him. He alone holds the floor on the matter of our mortality. "Because I live, you also will live."[125]

After two years of ministering to my old, dying friend— my "Thursdays with Les"—I didn't cry one day beside his bed in intensive care the tragic words of Dylan Thomas, "Rage, rage against the dying of the light." Instead I said: "You go, Les"; "We'll see you soon enough"; "God has forgiven all your sins, Les"; "Fly home to Jesus."

And when I lay myself down in death, I'll remember the One who said "Don't cry" to a woman who grieved for an only son. By the grace of God and not without it, I'll show my loved ones the meaning of ultimate spiritual freedom.

I'll put my hope in God and in the words I too will be waiting to hear: "Young man, I say to you, *get up!*"

What is sown in sorrow is raised in joy. This is God's promise. So we plant our loved ones like seed in the soil, with the faith any farmer has.

"I am the resurrection and the life."[126] That's what Jesus said. And the Christian, when reduced by death to what it really means to be one, savors these words. They hold us together.

"I want my freedom from all your rules"

Do you crave freedom from the impositions of the Christian God so that you might live as you please? Do you declare your independence from the ethical principles of Christianity? Do you know what you are asking for?

Does a triangle yearn to break free from the prison of its three sides? If it did, would it still be a triangle? We are objects of divine love, made to worship God and to love one another. This is our definition. Should we ask to be released from it?

Do trains wish to shake off the limitations of the rails and be free to go wherever they like? When it comes to trains, the tracks *are* freedom. To abandon them means crumpled metal in blackening flames. The whole countryside has been theirs. Not anymore.

Do sheep elect to shake off the safety of the shepherd's staff? Sure they do. But are they equipped for the barren, rocky spaces? Are they prepared for the mountain lions and the wolves? Do they not find thirsty or bloody deaths where they go looking for real and robust lives?

Unlock the metaphor Jesus created as he scanned the desperate, candlelit faces in the upper room. Is it in any sense freeing for branches to be cut off from their vine? I suppose such branches could go wherever they would want. Each could pretty much turn brown and die in any place it would like. I pick up the dead branches in my yard and throw them in the bonfire.

This is freedom?

Is it sweet liberation to abandon the very purpose of our existence . . . to leave the good and wholesome path God has prepared . . . to exchange eternal safety for destruction . . . to say to the source of all life, all peace, all hope, "Well, looks like this is good-bye"?

Excuse me, but do you *want* to die?

"I am the vine; you are the branches," said the Christ.

"Remain in me."

(Please read John 15:1-8.)

"So it's either abstinence or marry one person for life? You're serious, aren't you?" "So you want to legislate the things that come out of my mouth as well as what I choose to put in it?" "I am to listen to every last inconvenient whisper of my conscience . . . and still try to get ahead in life?"

Christianity, at first glance, might seem to mean accepting a thicket of rules and limitations that make life a lot less manageable and a great deal less fun. And so, it looks about as attractive as slavery. You're rather proud to announce that you've done things that would have shocked your poor old grandmother. "That's how times have changed," you think, fairly certain that you, not Grandma, are the enlightened one, the liberated one.

I can just imagine what you would think if you knew my Aunt Marie. She was up before the sun to make a breakfast for her husband so he could milk the cows . . . every day . . . for decades. Her life of duty and self-discipline would seem oppressive to you, at best. You look at her. You look at you. And you're happy to be free.

But let's talk about the word *slavery.*

To be a slave is to belong to someone else, in such a way that your will and desires are overruled. You lose your freedom of choice. You can't do what you want, go where you want, or have what you want. You do what you're told to do, though it is not in your own best interest. In fact, the very outcome of your life is up to the whims of someone else. That's what it means to be a slave.

The question is whether the life outside of Christ is really characterized by freedom or dreadful bondage.

Look into the eyes of the drug addict. How badly does she *not* want to do what she does? The ability to choose is nowhere in her. If anyone is a slave, she is. What you may not realize is that you may as well be looking into the eyes of any sinner. Friends, we cannot stop craving, lusting, competing, or pretending. We can't give up despising the people we don't need or disappointing those we do. We are not able to walk away from our self-centeredness, our greed, or our pride. We think we can stop sinning any time we want . . . until we once try. Then comes defeat. Then comes resignation. Then we look into the mirror and see a slave.

You say you *could* live a chaste, decent, holy life if you *wanted* to, but you *don't?* I understand that you like things as they are. I really do. Yet it is the ultimate in hopeless imprisonment when the slave prefers the chains and wouldn't leave, even if he could. Jesus had it right: "I tell you the truth, everyone who sins is a slave to sin."[127]

You are led unwillingly, inexorably to one appalling spot. I've seen you there already, crumbling beside the casket of someone you depended on, never to see him or her again. I've heard your hopeless weeping beyond the reaches of human comfort. You too are going to die. You have no choice; you will not be consulted in the matter at all. You pretend that it's okay with you, but this death is the curse that comes with sin. It is not okay. To be honest, you can't bear the thought, yet you can't stop thinking about it.

Enough. Now let's speak of freedom. Christianity is the very definition of the word, for *"if the Son sets you free, you will be free indeed."*[128]

First, there is freedom from the curse of sin, the "or else" that once hung over all our heads like a crushing hammer to punish us should we have failed in keeping a single righteous demand of God. It has been removed. To be more accurate, the hammer fell and fell hard on Christ, the Son of God. He became "a curse for us, for it is written: 'Cursed is everyone who is hung on a tree.' "[129] You are free the way a guilty criminal is free should the impossible verdict "not guilty" be handed down. Your verdict in Christ is an unforgettable moment of perfect quiet. A thousand demands ring in all our ears—"do more of this," "be more of that." But then they all fade away, leaving one exquisite command and only one: "Believe the good news. Christ has taken your sins away."

We have no righteousness of our own before God, no matter how slavishly we try to measure up to his holy demands. You have not lived until you've learned to say "Enough!" to the law that has shown you your guilt and so has done its work. You have not lived until you've just dismissed that law outright and have sent it away, until you've taken hold of Christ and the "the righteousness that comes from God and is by faith."[130] You haven't lived until you've come to know the sweet release that is the forgiveness of sins, release from your whole past and from the hopeless obligation to make it right somehow. It is an anchor cut loose, the surface of the water broken, and lungs filling with fresh air.

Second, though we will still endure a moment of physical death (unless Christ returns first), there is freedom from eternal death. You never need to experience that everlasting separation from God that was the consequence of our common rebellion against him. Freedom is my good friend Joe when he first discovered the grace of God. He saw his first glimpse of what Jesus Christ means to a mortal man, and he still loves to tell the new and unimagined thought that first visited him as he stepped out into the sun: "I looked up . . . and knew that I would never die."

One of my family's fond stories tells how my Aunt Marie exasperated the doctor who told her she had cancer. "All right," she said in response. And the doctor was sure she hadn't comprehended, so he told her again, more bluntly. "It's okay," she replied. So he became more and more persistent in the face of her maddening denial. "You are going to die!" he cried, so sure that *she* was the one that just didn't get it. She sighed, "That's fine."

Freedom.

And I remember the hired hands standing at her casket. They may have worked on Harvey and Marie's farm a decade before, but they came back for this. To see their shoulders shake at my Aunt Marie's casket, well, it made an impression on a little kid. But the comfort for this grief, the freedom for these tears, is just as available as faith. "Because I live, you also will live,"[131] said Jesus. You are not free to really live until you've seen death smile at you and you have smiled back through the hope you have in Jesus.

Third, you need to take another look at my Aunt Marie frying bacon at the stove with a sunrise still two hours away. What if this was her own deep desire? Did you ever think of that? What if it was her fondest wish to love her husband well, just as God in Christ loved her? What if, in the paradoxical phrase of Martin Luther, she was "loving Jesus and doing *whatever she wanted*"?

God wants no unwilling service. His desire is never to coerce us to do things we have no heart to do. No one can *force* you to do what, in your hearts of hearts, you really *want* to do. The grace of God causes new and holy desires, godly desires that are alive and well, to stir hidden beneath all that is merely human in every Christian. We see the human need all around, like a bottomless pit, knowing that when we've done all we can do, it will still be there just as before. So much need. But we are not overwhelmed. The abyss of human need belongs to Christ. It is his to fill. Our parts, our new desires are only to faithfully pour ourselves in.

To love a spouse well. To be fully present for your children. To see each day's circumstances and choices, obligations and demands for what they actually are—nothing more and nothing less than the daily raw material out of which you will fashion for God one faithful life for his honor. Why? Because these are the rules? No, that's not the mind of a Christian. "I want to know Christ."[132]

This is freedom, to feel the first stirrings of true worship and to find you are learning to love from the way he first loved you. You are finally yourself. You are finally alive.

A new life gradually taking its shape.

A train restored and set back on its track.

A lamb not forgotten, not ever let go.

A branch knit ever more tightly to a vine.

Martin Luther said, "Thinking must be turned in another direction, and Christ must be thought of that you may say: Christ lives."[133] Learn to live in deliberate, conscious awareness of the staggering grace of God . . . and you will be free indeed.

For the rules are transcended in a Relationship. The path turns out to be a Person. And all the ethical demands dissolve into one gracious imperative that releases its life within us and sets us free at last. "Remain in me," said Jesus, who loves us, who forgives us, who waits for us. For hearts can do no better that this.

"Only remain in me."

"Christianity is so antiwoman"

A mother came to Jesus. Her daughter was engaged in the battle of her life, "suffering terribly" at the hands of a cowardly demon. She came in the sincerity of a mom who would do anything for her little girl. "Lord, Son of David, have mercy on me!"

What this mother seemed to find when she met Jesus is a parallel to what many women today may think they see in any orthodox Christian church, namely, that they are dismissed. The all-male clergy looks suspiciously like an old boys' club. It feels to many women like an institutional insult against their very femaleness, and the slight turns out to be as old as church history.

It is very possible that when women join the work force, they see men at their worst. When women come to church, it may look like more of the same.

Think what happened to the poor woman in Matthew chapter 15. She wasn't dismissed by the Christian church but by Christ himself. When her need was desperate, the face he displayed was that of man utterly unwilling to help. "Sorry, wrong sex," said the times and the culture. "Wrong race," explained Jesus.

"I was sent only to the lost sheep of Israel."

"Lord, help me!" she said. By this time she was on her knees.

He put her off again, this time with an analogy in which the Jews were children at a dinner table, his saving help was their bread . . . and she was their dog.

Could he be more condescending? Is this not the sound of a door slamming shut and the sound of bolting and double bolting on the other side? By all appearances, by his own words, the Lord cared nothing for this woman, this mom.

But she knew him better than that!

She wrestled face-to-face with God in the muscular spirit of Jacob—"I won't let you go until you bless me"— and said: "Then a crumb, Lord! Give this dog a crumb!"

And the face he had been showing her changed.

The Jesus who seemed not to care let go the façade. The test was over. The essential kindness of God burst out toward the woman who bore the seeming insult.

She saw through him. She saw to his heart.

"Lord, you are good, no matter how you seem in my foolish pride. You care about me in a way no one else does. I will seek your face until I find it. I will pray as long as I have to—you will give in before I do! I am *not* going to go away. I have no one else!"

And Jesus was pleased.

"Woman, you have great faith!"

(Please read Matthew 15:21-28.)

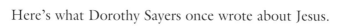

Here's what Dorothy Sayers once wrote about Jesus.

Perhaps it is no wonder that the women were first at the Cradle and last at the Cross. They had never known a man like this Man . . . a prophet who never nagged at them, who never flattered or coaxed or patronized, never treated them as 'the women, God help us!' or 'The ladies, God bless them!,' who rebuked and praised without condescension, who took their questions and arguments seriously. There is no act, no sermon, no parable in the whole gospel that borrows its pungency from female perversity. They had never known a man like this![134]

The Christian church is out of step with society on the topic of gender, and it will be important for you to come to terms with that. What will make all the difference is that you must deal with Christ first. What do you see *in Jesus* regarding his point of view toward women?

Observe a first century rabbi who engages in challenging dialogue with women. Draw close to a first century man whose greatest delight and richest compliments are likely to fall on women. Meet the One who comes to Mary's strong defense when all the disciples are against her. (And he certainly still rebukes men who do not have his heart when it comes to the place of women in his kingdom—all the times and places a woman was silenced when she did not need to be, when it would have been so much better to hear her voice.) See a living Savior, risen from the dead, who chooses to reveal himself first to women . . . and to let the first century men believe the testimony of women or continue on in despair. Jesus *is* different!

Then why 12 male apostles? Why rest authority in his church on men? The answer can't be that he was bound by the cultural norms of his own time and place. Clearly he wasn't. And women are not somehow incapable of leading. Then why?

It seems fairly obvious that for all of human history and in every society we can think of, men and women have found it natural to fall into different roles. It just seems to happen that way, over and over and over. Men certainly do abuse their power; women certainly can resent their positions. Both of these occurrences are bad. But the question is whether or not this recurring situation in which men and women play different parts is a show gone wrong from the start. On the strength of Scripture, I believe, instead, that a very good and beautiful thing has been twisted and corrupted.

The real truth is not that there *are* no roles but that we've forgotten how to wear them and that they're only ugly and oppressive because we see them and make them that way. The relationship between men and women is yet one more thing needing to be redeemed and restored in Christ.

The Christian ideal is simply that men and women are created equal but different. Different in ways intended to bless them. This reality is more beautiful than the notion of men and women as interchangeable. It is lovely in the way a couple carried along in the rhythm of a ballroom dance is lovely and the sound of bickering newlyweds jockeying for power is not. When they dance, each is equally indispensable. And although one leads and one follows, look again, because this is the very opposite of grim-faced competition. The harmonious fitting together of male and female can only happen or even make sense in Christ, where human pride and self-centeredness are properly dealt with. Human ego is always wanting to cut in. Jesus' own humility and grace create the rhythm that only the humble and broken and rejoicing hearts can hear.

Yes, the church is to be more like a dance than a factory or a political party. It is the one place in this world where the difference between men and women—the fact that their souls and spirits complete each other, just as their bodies do—can be celebrated and enjoyed. It is the one place where the question, Who's the best? sounds appropriately silly; where the dreadful business of being sure you're "getting your due" can be set down like the dead thing it is; where the question of status is left far behind—where we are nothing in ourselves and everything in Christ. It is an upside-down place where the one who wants to be the greatest must be the servant of all. This place is wherever Christ's influence is felt—the Christian home or the Christian church.

At very least, please give Christianity credit for the lovely truth it unveiled before the world centuries ahead of its time, the central tenet that men and women enjoy equal status before God and in Christ's church. Period. Men and women were equally created in God's image and were equally and tragically corrupted because of sin, but now they stand side by side in the gift of their redemption. This point needs to be understood and embraced before it is safe to return to the matter of roles, so I do hope you've got it.

Men and women enjoy full equality of status in the Christian church.

"There is neither . . . male nor female, for you are all one in Christ Jesus."[135]

As to the different roles that men and women are given to play, the woman's role can be called *helper,* a word that implies no inferiority—God himself is not ashamed to wear it.[136] Her submission is not a forced submission. To *submit* means that she willingly yields to her husband from a position of strength and out of the security she has in Christ. Such a submission isn't real, in the biblical sense, unless it's freely chosen. She *helps* him to be a man with her respect and admiration, just as he leads her to relax in his presence by being her strong advocate and the one who treasures her. That role, the man's, is called *headship,* a word that does not imply superiority—God the Father is the "head" of his true equal, Christ.[137] Headship is meant to look something like Jesus on his knees washing the disciples' feet. A man is to love his wife just as Christ loved the church, calling her more important than himself, should it cost him his life. When godly men lead their families and their churches in this same humble, sacrificial spirit, the wisdom and blessings of God will take their breath (and every complaint) away.

If the role of women often involves nurturing families and raising children, I agree with Chesterton that I can feel bad for women because of the *enormity* of the task and the *difficulty* of sacrificing other ambitions on the good altar of motherhood, but not because of the role's *insignificance*. Never that.

There's giggling in the next room. Always giggling. There my bride chatters away with my girls—about coupons, about tulip bulbs, about Jesus, about angels, about our Father, about carpet samples—and I wonder. What in this whole world matters more than what she does? "She is worth far more than rubies."[138] Who will better prepare my little girls to become Supreme Court justices or successful entrepreneurs or . . . just think . . . mommies?

To the charge of sexism, or even of condescension, I plead not guilty. God himself has taught us to call him Father—blessed be his name—and to see Christ as the Bridegroom and the church as his holy, beaming bride. Male and female are more than biological facts; they are shadows of unchangeable realities and of lovely unutterable mysteries. The argument for gender neutrality is not an argument in favor of equality but an argument against the church herself.

I'm not saying it's easy. Perhaps the time has come in my humble book to say that it's okay if all of your questions aren't answered to your satisfaction right now, today. It may be the doctrine of hell, the problem of pain, the challenge of science, or it may well be this bit about the roles of men and women that makes you say something like: "This is just a tough one for me. I want to know more about this Jesus. There's too much to lose to just walk away because of a single issue, no matter how jarring it is to me. Anyway, something I can't fully name won't let me walk away. So I'm just going to have to suspend judgment for the time being, keep listening, keep praying, and come back to this another time." That really is okay.

In other words, please don't let the defining question of your life—*Will you return the love of Love itself, for that is who God is?*—hinge on one answer that doesn't immediately satisfy or on one look you see on the divine face that you don't quite understand. The hope I hold out to you comes from some particularly strong, successful women I've been privileged to know, women who have taken the journey from being offended . . . to grudgingly accepting . . . to being profoundly moved by the scriptural teaching about women and men. It just took a little time.

First, these women needed the Spirit-worked confidence, authored at an empty grave, that everything that comes from the Father by his Word is good and is meant to bless. They needed the sweet Spirit-filled release of the soul submitting to Christ and his Word, longing to follow *wherever* he might lead, not because they were timid and not because someone said they had to but because he surrendered his all for them.

And if they seemed for a time to be receiving an insult from Christ, well, they now know him better than that.

Look into the face of Jesus . . . as he looks into the faces of women.

This is important, so please take the time. What do you see in John chapter 8 or in Matthew chapter 26, Luke chapter 7 or John chapter 20? You'll find in this order:

Forgiveness.

A strong defender.

He makes a woman's life unforgettable.

Her soul is safe with him.

"You just need life to mean something . . . it doesn't"

John the Baptist was doing hard time in prison when he sent two disciples to Jesus carrying the only question that mattered anymore. But the question was barbed like a fishhook. "Are you the one who was to come, or should we expect someone else?"

I, for one, do not think less of John for asking. (Neither did Jesus who, *after* fielding the question, took pride in his friend: "There is no one greater than John.")

Put yourself in John's sandals. For all his tireless work, where did he find himself? He was alone, in a dungeon, in the dark, and in pain. He wasn't asking to be relieved of his present misery or spared of his impending death. And Jesus did not offer to do these things. But as someone has said, "When we know the *why* in life, we can handle any *what.*"

John's "what" could have made the strongest heart fail.

His "why" was all wrapped up in Jesus.

If Christ is false, then there was no reason John should have been in that dungeon, in that darkness, always a few seconds from brutal death at the whim of unfeeling women and men. Ah, but if Christ is true . . .

If Jesus *is* the Son of God, then John's own life, every bit of it— from celebrated prophet to lonely prison dweller—was lived according to an eternal, good purpose. All of John's life mattered to the ultimate Someone. John had pointed to the Rabbi at the fringe of the crowd, crying, "Look, the Lamb of God," and there had been no mistake.

John knew that. Of course he did. I think he just wanted to hear it, that's all.

"Are you the one?"

And beyond what I can explain, I am stirred by the strength of Jesus' response: "Go back and report to John what you have seen and heard: The blind receive sight, the lame walk, those who have leprosy are cured, the deaf hear, the dead are raised, and the good news is preached to the poor."

I imagine John mustering all his strength just to lift his head and catch his disciples' words drifting down from above: "John, you should see the things he does. When he touches lepers, he doesn't catch their disease. They catch perfect healing. Lame men are dancing to the song the blind sing: 'I can see. I can see. Praise God, I can see.' Once-dead sons and daughters breathe and open their eyes and answer those who were crying out their names. Jesus wades into a sea of misery, leaving joy in his wake. He looks into desperate, impoverished eyes, and John, the news is always good. Always."

So then . . . he is the One.

I can only see John smiling as he rested his head back on the stone platter. In a little while, he would hear the only words that could have possibly mattered to him anymore: *"Well done."*

(Please read Luke 7:18-28.)

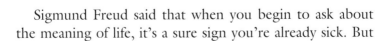

Sigmund Freud said that when you begin to ask about the meaning of life, it's a sure sign you're already sick. But this doesn't ring true. It is better to say that not only a wholesome mind but survival itself is at stake when a person asks: "What is life for? Does it mean anything after all?"

In a Nazi concentration camp, inmate Victor Frankl observed that it was precisely those prisoners who found a purpose in the midst of misery who were able to survive their horrifying conditions. Those who responded with human compassion to the suffering they saw transcended their own suffering. Those who lost themselves in a reason bigger than themselves lived. Those who didn't see a point for the next day, who couldn't find good reasons to breathe the next breath, well . . . they didn't.

Thus, this notion about needing to know the *why* so as to survive any *what* was born and tested in the most extreme conditions, and indeed, became the basis of a radical new form of psychotherapy. Frankl discovered that he could free people from neurosis not by focusing on their problems, which only served to energize their painful, distorted thoughts, but by helping them find some meaning larger and truer than those problems.

Why, after all, does a woman who loses a child to a drunk driver found a national organization called Mothers Against Drunk Driving? She grasps for meaning in the gut-punching pain, and humanly speaking, she does it to survive.

So do we all. Who can argue with the fact that some sort of ultimate meaning is necessary for the significance we all hunger for? Somehow we and our tiny contribution must last, for if in the end we are nothing, neither existing ourselves nor even held in the memory of a single mind, we are *next* to nothing already. The existential philosophers opine that life is about knowing there is no such meaning. They instruct us to face the fact that there is no larger purpose. So we are told to make our courageous, irrational decision *to be* anyway, in the face of ultimate despair. They say there is no such future and no such Person as ultimate meaning depends on . . . so salute the sinking ship . . . or go down below for a last hand at poker . . . it matters not. But pretend it does.

Thank you, existentialism. That helps a lot.

It reminds me of Soren Kierkegaard's comments about the philosopher who explained everything in life . . . except how to get through an ordinary day. Getting through an ordinary day is precisely the task many are not up to. Their sense of wonder has drowned in their consuming sense of self. How many people are deciding right now that this day is their last? They are as weary of pleasure as they are of pain, and their minds are empty of any compelling motive to go on.

In other words, nihilism, thanks for nothing.

Hear the unblushing confession of skeptic Aldous Huxley: "I had *motives* for not wanting the world to have meaning." He admitted that he was merely preserving the freedom, so-called, to indulge his cravings without restraint. It was as simple as that. As to how such beliefs are formed, it's enough for some people that they don't *want* to go to church, don't *want* every child to be carried to term, don't *want* to stick with one spouse. Huxley continued, "Those who detect no meaning in the world generally do so because, for one reason or another, it suits their books that the world should be meaningless."[139] To abandon us all to this nightmarish world where nothing matters suits their books?

While today's sophisticates have largely abandoned the question of meaning, that doesn't mean the question has gone away. The truth is, nothing can prevent human beings from clamoring to know that they matter, that they are significant, that they have had some sort of impact, and that they have made some difference to someone. *To Someone.*

As relational beings, every person instinctively knows that whatever the meaning of life is, love is near the center of it. As Christopher Morley said, "If we all discovered that we had only five minutes left to say all that we wanted to say, every telephone booth in the world would be occupied by people calling other people to stammer that we love them."[140] We each have to matter to someone besides ourselves. Who will remember us? Anyone?

And we all secretly know that the hunger for significance is no neurosis. It is a legitimate human desire. And while philosophy shrugs its shoulders over that need as a psychological curiosity along with hope and along with wonder, Christianity fully validates it and speaks into it with simple eloquence: "Whatever you did for one of the least of these brothers of mine, you did for me."[141]

According to Christianity, these are the words of the Ultimate Person; these are the words of Christ. When we listen to him, we listen to God. To know his rejection because of all the life we spent on ourselves and on our own worthless purposes is, quite simply, to wither and die. Conversely, to know his delight, by grace, is to live life in the firm grip of reality. Don't miss the meaning in all Jesus' talk of little things like cups of water and humble servanthood for his sake. "Your life has meaning, because it means something to me. Nothing done for me is ever forgotten. It lasts and lasts and lasts precisely because I do. So do you, together with me. *We* last." Do you see? The One who lives forever lives to remember you. This is meaningful. There is nothing else.

When former Chrysler C.E.O. Lee Iaccoca was reminiscing about his celebrated achievements in his book *Talking Straight*, he made a startling confession about all his fabulous successes. "Here I am in the twilight of my years, still wondering what it is all about. I can tell you this. Fame and fortune are for the birds." He was echoing the sentiments of Solomon who had "had it all" three millennia earlier: *"Meaningless, a chasing after the wind."*[142] And Iaccoca went on. "Fame and fortune are for the birds. Then I look at my children . . . *and I love them.*"[143]

It's the sound of a seismic shift taking place at a man's foundation. "I used to live *for that* . . . now I live *for this.*"

His words are compelling. However, Iaccoca does his children no favor, given the tragic flaw in us all, when he makes them his new center, telling them that now his happiness depends on them. There is only one up to the task of supplying meaning or satisfying the hunger for significance.

I look at Jesus dying for me, rising for me. I know who he is. *And I love him.*

And I know what my life is: from you, for you, to you, my dear God.

To trust him is the alternative to despair. To love as we are loved is to move from the fringes of life toward the center. To worship the perpetual novelty of our God is our very reason for living, the unifying principle of the universe. No amount of philosophizing can displace the imperatives.

> Let the sea resound, and everything in it,
>   the world, and all who live in it.
> Let the rivers clap their hands,
>   let the mountains sing together for joy.[144]

To the question of identity, Dietrich Bonhoeffer wrote, "Who am I? Whoever I am, thou knowest, O God. I am thine."[145] Every other answer to that nagging Who *am* I? will fade to insignificance. I am . . . I am . . . and you fill in the blank with your calling, your culture, your best achievement, your greatest ability, how good you look, or your favorite thing to do. But these will be stripped away from you, one by one, as your life inevitably diminishes. None of these are forever. None of these are anything at all next to God.

Who are you? *You are his.*

What matters even now is not how popular or successful you are, who notices you, or if anyone ever does . . . but whom you serve. Your why is all wrapped up in Christ.

It's an exquisite image from a classic story. The old juggler—used up, spent, and long since forgotten by the crowd—slips unnoticed into the cathedral. He stands alone in front of the altar, in front of the One, with candlelight flickering in his eyes.

All is still until the perfect quiet is punctuated by the quiet, rhythmic slapping of juggling pins on palms . . . and tears stream down his face. "If I am nothing but a juggler . . . then let me juggle for you." This is meaning, O Lord, to know how you love me, to take what I've been given to do, and do it for the love of you.

"You're going to want me to evangelize?"

What did Jesus see in Zacchaeus?

A pathetic, small man in the crook of a tree? A scoundrel in a nice pair of shoes?

I suppose what Jesus saw was need—raw, desperate, eternal need. A dead-man-walking needing to be made alive. A hell-bound soul wanting rescue. A billion-of-a-kind sinner needing to be changed. So much need perched up in a sycamore tree— the very type of need that drew the Son of God from eternity into time and toward a tree of his own.

Was Zacchaeus conscious of all that he needed? Did he wake up that morning and say, "If I died tonight, where would I be?" Not likely. For many, such matters are hidden below the waterline of conscious thought. The stuff of dreams . . . bad ones. No, he may not have understood the eternal issues that swirled in the breeze around his tax-collecting booth, that brought the Savior to his town. Still, *something* made Zacchaeus climb that tree for just a passing glimpse of Christ. Some isolation. Some inadequacy. Some tightness in his chest. Jesus saw the deficiency for what it was— a place to start.

These are the places Jesus touched people first: the hand

that was withered, the back that wouldn't straighten, the stomach that was hungry. He met people at the level of their present distress, at the spot where a child lay dead or a crippled man sat and begged.

"What do you want?" he asked a blind man, and he was not offended at the answer.

"I want to see." Of course. "I don't want to feel along the wall for the best place to grovel. I want to fill my time with manly work and manly rest. I want to know the sights that fit with the sounds of children laughing and rain falling. I want to see."

"Then you shall see."

People brought Jesus their needs, and he did what he could. It wasn't the best he had to offer when he merely healed their bodies or filled their stomachs; the best he could give was his own self in exchange for their guilty souls. Still, he looked up at a sycamore tree and the loneliness in its branches and knew what to say.

"Zacchaeus, I must stay at your house today." So simple . . . but how it must have sounded to that sad little man. Acceptance. "You think no one would want to spend time with you? I would. You're sure no one notices you? Well, guess what? I do."

Put yourself in the little shoes of Zacchaeus, watching Jesus over the heads of the suffocating crowd as he clears a path toward you, seeing the one everyone wants to get close to wanting to get close to you. Tonight your house will be a temple. Soon your Lord will ascend his tree. And a little human kindness on the part of the Son of God was the key that fit the lock. Now what does Jesus see?

He sees Zacchaeus, the IRS agent of his day, smiling . . . giving everything . . . confessing all.

He sees a newly enlarged man squeezing through the eye of a needle. Someone who was long lost is suddenly, finally found.

(Please read Luke 19:1-10.)

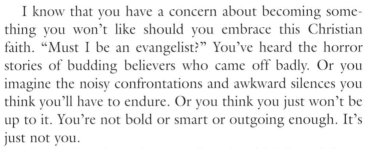

I know that you have a concern about becoming something you won't like should you embrace this Christian faith. "Must I be an evangelist?" You've heard the horror stories of budding believers who came off badly. Or you imagine the noisy confrontations and awkward silences you think you'll have to endure. Or you think you just won't be up to it. You're not bold or smart or outgoing enough. It's just not you.

If so, look again at the story above in which Jesus "shares Jesus" with Zacchaeus. There are no quick retorts. No angry confrontations. Nothing particularly clever. What was it like being on either side of that exchange of grace? Enviable! Trust me. It's just a man finding out he's loved by God in a way no one else ever could. That's all.

You're not thinking of witnessing clearly enough until you're trying to imagine the gratification of responding to people in the realm of deepest need. You may not have the gift to debate with angry or complacent skeptics. That's really okay. But there are people whom you will meet, not in moments of controversy but in moments of hurt. I speak of the "low hanging fruit" so dear to God. They do not put up bitter resistance; they reveal a place beneath their surfaces where they are not doing nearly so well as they let on. Think of plaintive eyes looking to you, wondering if you have anything to say. Soon, very soon, if you come to know Jesus, you will have plenty to say. The moments are prepared, as are the words.

"For God so loved the world . . ."

Just the simple healing truth wrapped in simple human kindness.

You can't see it now, but giving away what you find in him may be the very highlight of your life. Though it is more humbling than I can say, I recall the appreciation I've received from people with whom I, though fumbling around, managed to share Christ. I remember the way they looked at me, the things they said that were far *too much:* "God sent you to me," the woman said. "I was about to kill myself . . . the sleeping pills were in my hand . . . until I thought of what you taught me." Or the note in a fifth grader's scribble that said: "I saw you there after my dad's funeral. You looked like Jesus with your arms opened wide. I knew it was going to be okay." What it means to me to remember that woman now, what it feels like to read that note . . . is what I want you to know.

"Be active in sharing your faith," the apostle Paul once wrote to Philemon, and you will understand "every good thing we have in Christ."[146] As the words show up on your own lips, you best find out all that God gave to his world when he gave Jesus. In always new and deeper ways, you make Jesus your own.

There's more. Christ promises spiritual gifts to all who know him. For some, they will speak simple words of faith, thinking *anyone* could say these things, but when *they* say them, people tear up or are deeply encouraged or suddenly understand. Others find in themselves refreshing new desires to pour themselves out in service, curious longings, just once, to wash someone else's feet. Do it all? Do things for which you aren't equipped? No. It's liberating to know that there will be something for you to do, which, when you do it, will feel like a puzzle piece falling at last into place. "What I've given you . . . what I've *made* you to do . . . *you* and no one else . . . *do that!*"

But bring people to Christ? Me? Here's a bit of advice in just four steps.

One: "Open your eyes."[147]

That's what Jesus said. You are merely asked to keep your
eyes open for people in your life, in your circle of influence,
who need to know what you've found in him. Don't overlook the people whom you see all the time: those who bring
you coffee, who do your hair, who work at the next cubicle,
who sit across from you at the dinner table, whom you've
just met, whom you've known all your life. Don't overlook
the ones everyone else does: those too different, too shy, too
together, too needy. Is there someone in your life with a
new interest in spiritual things or an interest in a deeper
friendship with you? Open your eyes.

Two: "Pray . . . that God may open a door for [the]
message."[148]

There is something that must come in between identify-
ing a person in need of Christ and saying your first hesitant
words, and it makes all the difference. Mention the person's
name to God. Remind yourself to pray about him or her
continually. Let the reminder be a red thread around your
finger or a 3 x 5 inch card on your dashboard. Let the prayer
go something like this: "Heavenly Father, it's just me again,
praying for Joe. I know the immensity of what I'm asking
you and how audacious this prayer would sound if you
weren't truly my Father. But please, use me to bring Joe to
you. Let me display to him something of Jesus when I see
him. And make my joy complete by making him yours in
Christ. Amen."

Three: Be an "imitator of God"[149] through some act of
human kindness.

Do you know how Jesus pictures the Last Day? He will
waste no time in rewarding people for the things they did
"for one of the least of these brothers." He will say:
"Remember those things you did? No? Well, I do . . .
because you did them for me." What things? Little things
really, like giving someone a drink or a bite to eat, showing
kindness to a stranger, giving away a shirt (pretending it

doesn't fit anymore), or spending a little time with the sick (including the sick at heart). Taking time. Lifting a burden. Lending a hand. No Ph.D. required. No need for a committee. Don't bother calling the newspaper. The memories Jesus will savor on that day don't require advanced knowledge, honed skills, or a single spectator besides, of course, himself. Only care for others the way he cares for you. The most modern postmodern person may find radical love in Jesus' name difficult to dismiss.

Four: "Speak the truth in love."[150]

From the time you become a Christian, you'll want to begin thinking through how you will clearly articulate the simple message of Christ: Why we need him. Who he is. What he did. What it means. There is no need at all for arm twisting. There is no pressure to "close the sale." You just tell what you know. You are simply a plain-spoken *witness* of the way God saved the world in Christ. Nothing more. Nothing less.

And while you're growing up in the ability to speak freely and openly about Jesus, what you certainly can do is extend the openhearted invitation for someone, anyone, to join you in whatever sacred place you go to learn about and worship Christ. Jesus told a story in which the kingdom of God was portrayed as a banquet held by a king. The king's persistent invitation is the key feature of the story. He invites and invites . . . *and then invites again.* Imagine. We could be made to plead and grovel, scratch and claw our entire lives, begging to be let in to the presence of a celebrating God. But it's God who does that asking! *"Come to the wedding banquet of my Son."* Since we have been married (inseparable and eternally bonded) to God's Son by faith and now feast on the banquet of his grace, the invitation goes out through us. "The Spirit and the bride"—that's us—"say, 'Come!'"[151] Be winsome and confident, not shy or apologetic. "Joe, I'd just really like you to come to church with me." And remember, you are doing a very good thing.

I know. I know. Part of you wants to say that you don't know enough of the Bible yet to share your new faith or that you're life isn't together enough to be Christ's representative. But while we are in this world, we will always be God's unfinished work, mere beginners, wounded healers, childlike teachers. Though God is not finished with us, we who are in Christ are in possession of the wisdom of the universe, and we do know what to say: *"For God so loved the world . . ."*

They don't know if there's a heaven. They're a little fuzzy on the subject of God. They certainly do not want to be notches on some evangelist's belt. But all people hurt. All people worry. All people want to be loved.

Do you see a colleague sorrowing in a new world of grief? Do you see how the neighbor boy watches you . . . and how no dad is ever around? Do you see the outcast dying quietly at the edge of the party?

Do you see . . . a place to start?

"Why go through the motions of prayer and worship?"

Jesus stood up to read the Scripture at the synagogue in his hometown. He chose a seven-century-old text that dripped with the longing of the prophet Isaiah. He looked for a beautiful, inevitable "some day" called the year of the Lord's favor. And as Jesus began to expound on those words, the first word he uttered was *today.*

"Today this Scripture is fulfilled."

+   +   +

Nicodemus was afraid and confused. His fear had to do with the people he ran with and what they would think of him now, sneaking off under the cover of darkness just to look into the face of the Rabbi from Galilee. His confusion had to do with the Miracle Worker himself and just exactly how one was to enter this "kingdom of God" he spoke about. Was it by obedience? by moral effort? by strong decision? How?

"[By] water and the Spirit," Jesus told him.

+   +   +

Some three years later came Jesus' Last Supper. This was the night in which the Old Testament gave way to the New, when the old focal point in God's household—an altar gruesomely spattered with blood—was replaced with the intimacy and welcome of a table where Jesus served a meal that was himself. He broke the bread and passed it around, labeling it "My body." And the wine the disciples drank from one cup was "My blood." To this table we are to bring ourselves again and again and again.

"In remembrance of me," Jesus said.

+   +   +

Speaking the Word, sprinkling the water, breaking the bread, and passing out the wine—these are the kinds of things Philip Yancey referred to as "Jesus . . . just being Jesus." This is what makes us rise to our feet for the reading of the gospel just as we always have, why we lean forward and get quiet to hear the splash of water and to see a baby wake up, why we stand in line for our bit of bread and wine, the "I have so loved you" we can taste and touch. We've done these things from the beginning, and we will do them to the end.

We are, after all, the church . . . just being the church.

(Please read Luke 4:14-21; John 3:1-21; and Luke 22:19-22.)

Do the Christian rituals of repeated prayers and predictable worship become empty of meaning after a while? If so, just where does the problem lie?

I've been saying grace since I was a little boy. Before a meal we sometimes prayed a verse from the Psalms: "The eyes of all wait upon thee; and thou givest them their meat in due season. Thou openest thine hand, and satisfiest the desire of every living thing."[152] It put a good picture in my young mind of bunnies and squirrels with their faces cocked toward the sky. If I ever felt invincible as a child, this prayer told me that I was a tiny creature after all and that I needed God. Our naked, raw dependence goes this far: God turns the brown field green again and again and again . . . or else we die.

Sometimes, though, let's face it. The food sat there all steamy, and the prayer was a blur. A half hour later I would say, "Dad, may I please be excused?"

"I don't know . . . what did you do?" was the kidding answer. Then, "Let's return thanks." And if the prayer *before* dinner was rushed, it was nothing like what happened to the "Oh, give thanks unto the Lord. . . ." The way that verse released us we might as well have reverently closed our eyes and prayed, "On your marks . . . get set . . . go." By the time Dad opened his eyes, there were five little puffs of smoke where his children had been.

And yet if these brief Scriptures were sometimes thoughtlessly recited, it doesn't follow that we should stop saying them. Indeed, if the very deepest things that Christians act out when together—Baptism and Holy Communion— should ever leave us cold and unaffected, it doesn't mean it's the acts that need to be changed.

Clearly, if there's any dullness, it is in us.

My mind wanders back to the Last Supper of Christ. We're told that when the meal was over, he and the disciples sang a hymn. We are reasonably certain what hymn it was. The good Rabbi would not have let the Passover end without the traditional chanting of the "Hallel Psalms," numbering 115–118. Read the words for yourself, and juxtapose them against that night in the upper room. "Why do the nations say, 'Where is their God?' "[153] sang Jesus, about to die for all. Pause, and take that in. Consider Christ chanting the night before his own personal hell: "The LORD is with me; I will not be afraid. *What can man do to me?*"[154] God only knows what ran through his mind.

And the very last words of the Last Supper's Hallel Psalms, words releasing them from that table where Jesus must have wanted to stay forever, were these: "Give thanks to the LORD, for he is good; his love endures forever."[155]

The Son of God was saying grace.

And with that he was released from the meal. Soon they would lay Jesus down on the wooden beams and position his limbs as needed. Someone would approach with a nail. He would open his hand . . . *"and satisfy the desires of every living thing."*[156]

My baptism, his Supper, the Scriptures of the ancient liturgy—far more than ritual, these are all designed to take me right back there, back to the grace. And no, it never gets old. *"His compassions . . . are new every morning; great is your faithfulness."*[157]

Allow a brief explanation of the unique things you'll encounter in a Lutheran worship service. Liturgy is a highly structured, thoughtfully ordered, deliberately transcendent style of worship. This is how the church "removes its shoes; the place on which she walks is holy ground."[158] We take up our new and refreshing fascination, no longer with ourselves but with the sort of God who would send his Son.

By design, the liturgy is built on Scripture out of the hard-won conviction that God's Word is the means through which he keeps us alive to him and he has his way with us to persuade us, move us, and change us. God's gift of music is a beautiful vehicle that carries God's Word to a deep place in each of us. Even when we don't feel in our soul every-thing David meant by his fervent prayer—*"Create in me a pure heart, O God . . . Do not . . . take your Holy Spirit from me"*[159]—at least it's how we want to feel . . . and even in this poor way we show that God is indeed drawing us closer to himself than we were before.

Further, when I sing, "O Christ, Lamb of God, you take away the sin of the world," I am blending my voice to the voices of the millions like me spread across the centuries. I am taking my place in the "one holy Christian and apostolic church," with her one foot on earth and one in heaven. However old age may whittle me down one day, whatever human capacities wither away, I'm counting on the liturgical words, the ones I've been singing all my life, to rise to the surface of me and carry me home.

> Lord, now you let your servant depart in peace according to your word. For my eyes have seen your salvation, which you have prepared before the face of all people, a light to lighten the Gentiles and the glory of your people Israel.

Embedded like jewels in the liturgy, if the worship service calls for one or the other, are the sacraments, the visible Word. Baptism and Holy Communion are the two sacred acts that are set apart from all the other rituals Christians perform. To understand them, you must understand that what creates and sustains faith are the objective promises of God in his Word. "I have reconciled you to myself." This is the gospel. It is the Good News of Jesus Christ. We recognize that same message—"I, your God, do not hold your sins against you"—connected to the water of Baptism and to the bread and the wine of Holy Communion. One time in each of our lives we get to feel that sweet absolution in the baptismal water running over our heads. In the mystery of the very real presence of Christ's body and blood in the bread and wine, we taste and touch the promise that God really has forgiven us for Jesus' sake. God's saving accomplishment on the cross is pronounced by Word and sacraments, so that we may keep believing that it is so. The sacraments do nothing less for us than keep our faith alive.

To be very clear then, here is why I go to church. I go to *exhale* my confession of sin, to expel my punctured conceit. I breathe out my hopes-turned-prayers, my songs of praise, my offerings of faith, my "I believe in God the Father Almighty . . . and in Jesus Christ his only Son. . . ." And when my pastor turns toward me, toward us, I inhale the Word from God and God's breathtaking worldview, and I breathe in deeply his timeless declaration of pardon, his guidance, his "This is my body . . . my blood . . . poured out for you," his benediction.

Perhaps what makes these forms of worship seem like "empty ritual" to some people is actually the fact that they are not emotionally manipulative . . . which is rather the beauty of it. God's forgiveness has an invaluable objective quality—it's true whether we feel it or not. For life in this world, such as it is, we need faith that doesn't rest on the shifting sands of our own religious feelings or the day-to-day changes in our personal experiences. We rest on the objective promises of God himself and on the salvation he set into the stone of unchangeable historical fact. This is the grace he speaks to us again and again and again in water and Word, in bread and wine.

"I forgive you."

And yet while we don't depend on human feeling to validate the things God says, don't think there is no feeling. Genuine Christian emotion and the lovely experiences of grace follow unforced, unearned as God chooses to provide them. For our part we keep the spotlight on the facts: Christ was born; Christ was crucified; Christ died; Christ is alive; Christ is coming again. Keep your eyes on these facts.

They will get up and dance.

As I set the well-worn verses against the backdrop of my life, the meanings pour out.

In my days of adolescent pain, the meals began: "The eyes of all wait upon thee, O Lord. . . . Thou openest thine hand and satisfiest the desires of every living thing."

I remember sitting with my bride at McDonald's the morning our first daughter was to be born. Before the big breakfast, we held hands and prayed: "Come, Lord Jesus, be our guest. Let these gifts to us be blessed."

I imagine the day I will bury a parent. We will gather for a meal when it's all over, and we'll almost certainly pray, "Give thanks to the LORD, for he is good. . . ."

And we'll mean it. God *is* good. We're released by these words in a way nothing else ever can release us.

"His love endures forever."

"All

the church

cares about

is money"

Mary broke her jar open, and along with it her tender spirit. Her perfume and her devotion poured out on Jesus' head and pooled at his feet, overwhelming the room. He saw to the soul of what she did and was pleased.

"She did it to prepare me for burial."[160]

For all the times he had tried to tell his followers that he was going to die for them and for all the times they had said, "No, Lord, it will never happen," it was only Mary that had really heard him.

And it tore her wide open.

You would think a hush would have fallen on the room. You would have expected a hush. But the rest of the story is all too predictable. As with the gleaming creation itself, it's just like Satan to pounce on something so new and so good. And Judas, so close by, was all too available.

"Why wasn't this perfume sold and the money given to the poor?" he cried.

On its surface, his criticism seemed aimed at Mary for her pointless waste of resources. If we didn't know Judas better, we would even hear a legitimate concern for the needy. But how often the worst things—intolerance, ambition, greed—disguise themselves as piety. We will see his true colors soon enough. He was trying to serve two masters at the same time, both money and Christ, but it was not working.

One he had come to despise.

We can hardly miss the implication in Judas' words, the thinly veiled stab, that Jesus wasn't worth the perfume.

What Jesus said to Martha who had once criticized Mary's devotion as well, what he had said to death, which had come for Mary's brother, he now says to Judas.

"Leave her alone!"

Then Jesus beamed at Mary—that it was *not* too much, that she would *never be forgotten,* that there is a time for breaking the jar. But Jesus' words for his critic, for the man with the dollar signs in his eyes, were as disturbing as words get.

"You will not always have me."

(Please read John 12:1-11.)

The usher is looking decidedly uncomfortable. The offering basket has hit a snag in the pew ahead of you. A boy is clutching a nickel in his chubby fist, which Mom is shaking over the basket. She peals back one finger at a time, whispering the sort of whisper that echoes around the sanctuary, "Let go!" Finally, the boy, desperate to know why God wants his money, releases the treasure. The nickel drops home, the usher relaxes . . . and God is five cents richer.

Just as there was a Judas among the first disciples of Jesus, there are those within the visible church who will do anything they can to get your nickel into the plate. Though I pray they are few, there are those who will lie to you, pressure you, and shame you for the sake of money. I make no apology for them. These things are shameful.

In none of these things do they represent Jesus. But how unreasonable it is to turn away from Jesus and his family of believers, of all things, because of Judas! More than unreasonable, it would be to your own terrible loss to do so.

Though I'll be the church's harshest critic when it is wrong, I've also seen the church in moments that have the same look and feel as the introductory story of Mary. She cared about money not at all. I've pressed five hundred dollars into a needy young couple's hands on an errand from someone "who wished to remain anonymous." The note read, "In Jesus' name," and I felt the beautiful joy of Jesus on both ends of the exchange. I grew up worshiping in an extravagantly beautiful church that some people may have said was too much. But that holy place rose up out of the soil of poor German immigrants who got by with less, a lot less, and called it a privilege to do such a thing for the glory of God. Jesus is worth it, so they "broke the jar," and it is beautiful in my eyes . . . and in the Lord's eyes.

In the introductory story, criticism about money comes from the very one who cares too much for the stuff himself, the one who stands outside of the heartbreaking devotion of Mary not understanding what he is looking at. While the church is open to criticism on this and any other issue and even a faithful church can now and then lose itself in merely institutional concerns, there are also very legitimate concerns about money that groups of people that mean to follow Jesus will inevitably share.

Any faithful church has a legitimate concern for spreading the message of Jesus. It is the church's mission, the very reason it lives and breathes, to tell the world about Christ at any cost. One of the costs happens to be money. In fact, this cost demonstrates what a wonderful gift money is for a church. Just think, this stuff we call money allows me to translate my time and work—that is, *myself*—into ministry. It's difficult to call lucre "filthy"[161] when you've seen it translated into awesome outreach moments in which people, even on the far side of the world, are hearing about the great love of Jesus.

But the church is also concerned that the motivation behind the giving of money is pristine, untouched by human pressure and joyless obligation. God wants no unwilling service, but he wants believers to give in cheerful response to the grace he has lavished so freely and outrageously on them. If you are a spiritual seeker, we only want you to come and listen. We don't want you to give a dime until you *want* to because of what you've heard, until the love of Christ compels you inwardly. God doesn't want your money. He wants you.

There's the rub. Does he have you? Any faithful church will have a legitimate concern for the worldly attachments people feel toward their money. "Where your treasure is, there your heart will be also,"[162] warned Jesus. The Bible cuts to the heart of what materialism really is, warning us not to put our "hope in wealth."[163] Please consider that defining phrase. Understand that materialism is not marked merely by the fact that we have lots of stuff. It is God who has so blessed us. Materialism is trying to meet *spiritual needs,* such as *hope,* by accumulating *material things,* such as *wealth.* Material needs for clothing, food, and shelter are appropriately met by material things. But the need to know that I'm someone, that I'm loved, that everything is well with my soul today and will be tomorrow, well, these are spiritual needs. Materialism is the way money makes promises—be it status or security, peace or joy—that only God can possibly keep.

"Hope in wealth." Material possessions connected to spiritual need—this is the very association virtually every television commercial is trying to make. If the advertisers can just get you to connect the car with the joy on that man's face, if they can just get you to believe that their cologne has something to do with love—that's materialism. For Pete's sake, they've even tried to associate Coca-Cola with world peace!

And we fall for it. That we do is written all over our faces as we take a new car for a test-drive. The man who just won it all on *Who Wants to Be a Millionaire* trembles for the very joy of it. Trembles! And we understand it. Clearly, wealth is one of the most potent of the false gods, a shameful source of misplaced devotion, which will end up breaking your heart in the end.

In the penetrating words of Jesus, "Life does not consist in the abundance of [your] possessions."[164] Mere things can never fill what philosopher Blaise Paschal termed the "God-shaped hole" in our hearts. And so the church, if it is to be faithful, must keep confronting the damnable idolatry and keep calling the love of money exactly what it is—the "root of all kinds of evil"[165]—to compel our repentance and to clear the center of our stage for the One who is alone worthy to be our Lord.

You see, it was not Mary, it was God himself who went too far, who went overboard when that which he broke and poured out completely was his only Son. But then the fragrance of "Father, forgive them" filled the world. With the soft cry of the new baby in Bethlehem and with the hours of agony on the cross, God was saying something to devils, to demons, and to death itself. It was God's settled determination to save the world, whatever the cost.

"Leave them alone!"

What is the faith that is "of greater worth than gold"?[166] It is in you, reading these words and hearing the news that comes so freely. It thinks to itself, "Then how blessed I am." You who now have the faith have taken hold of the *"life that is truly life."*[167] You've come to know the God who cares for you, who has carried you this far as on eagle's wings, and who blesses you with every spiritual blessing in the material, touchable, holdable Christ.

And that's when something happens that you hadn't expected while standing on Judas' side of the room instead

of Mary's. Your face brightens. *"We love,"* you finally understand, *"because he first loved us."*[168] And the death grip
miraculously loosens. Then comes an act that's born of a
freedom you never knew before, that is made of dependence, of trust, and of worship.

Your hand just opens.

On July 25, 2000, a little congregation in Rockford, Illinois, a church called New Life, "broke a jar."

It did something extravagant that the legalist will
never understand, something excessive for the prudent
to roundly criticize . . . which is kind of the beauty of it.
The congregation members gathered in their new sanctuary to worship.

But did they need to raise the cross 60 feet in the air?
Did there have to be a hardwood floor in the chancel
where carpet would have been fine? And what is the purpose of all that wasted space over their heads?

There is no purpose other than to honor Christ.

Yes, it cost a lot of money. But I preached to them that
if their hearts were right, crying, "He is worthy!" then this
place was holy oil poured out on the Savior's head, running down his face and pooling at his feet.

May all that God pours in as we listen to his Word pour
out of us. May his fragrance be on us. May our words be
extravagant, seeming to go too far and to say too much
that the God of heaven and earth loves us in Christ his Son.

"No one

believes

in sin

anymore"

If you have ever wondered why anyone would have wanted a nice man like Jesus dead, your answer can be heard, furious and shouting, in the gospel of Matthew, chapter 23. We call this scene the Seven Woes of Jesus.

Savor the bitter words. Read the pathos and pain between the lines when Love got up and told the truth in the temple courts at Jerusalem. The truth that those who thought themselves good people doing well were sinners living a split second from hell.

"How will you escape?" Christ bellowed.

For God is holy. God is unalterably just. And there is such a thing as sin.

So the solemn quiet of the temple courts was pierced by the seven bitter shrieks of desperate, good grief. "Woe to you!" That is to say: "Oh, be careful. If you only knew the holiness of God!"

Then, as suddenly as it began, the mighty thunder of Jesus turned to sorrowful rain. "Jerusalem, Jerusalem, how often I have longed to gather your children together . . ." He wanted the sinners anyway, even though they were what they were. The woes were wounds from a friend, the kind they could have trusted. They had lived to hear the Lion of Judah roaring in their temple courts on a holy weekday, setting dreadful things in motion, pushing the buttons that would get him killed, orchestrating his own death to occur on the Jewish Day of Preparation. That means Christ was calling out words like Father and forgive and finished even as ten thousand Passover lambs were crying in the holy city and in the temple courts, even as sheep blood flowed like a river down the jagged grooves of Mount Zion.

For the Lion became "the Lamb of God, who takes away the sin of the world."[169]

(Please read Matthew 23:1-39.)

I entered the work force as a seventh grader, earning peanuts at a garden nursery. One day I was carrying a wooden tray of carefully separated seedlings—cucumbers on one side, watermelons on the other. I managed to spill them all over the floor of the greenhouse. When I tried to reorganize the seedlings, they looked identical. I thought for half a second of telling my boss what I had done, but there was no way I saw that conversation going well. Before I knew it, a farmer's wife was asking for cucumber seedlings. And . . . well . . . I sort of *guessed.*

I've thought about those little seedlings many times over the years, reflecting deeply on the fact that watermelon seedlings inevitably grow up into the surprise of full-grown watermelons, no matter what anyone says or thinks about them. They become what they *have* to become, ignoring and denying all other beliefs to the contrary.

Call it the inexorable law of the farm. "God cannot be mocked," the Scriptures declare. "A man reaps what he sows. The one who sows to please his sinful nature, from that nature will reap destruction."[170] *We reap what we sow.*

People who deny the reality of sin do not exempt themselves from sin's natural consequences. If you don't know sin by a sensitive conscience anymore or by the dos and don'ts that were clear enough when you were small, then recognize sin by its results. Sow criticism into a marriage, anger into a childhood, lies into a friendship, sexual immorality into a life, and stand back to learn *the law of the farm.* Neglect to do good things that you know are yours to do—recall the words left unspoken, the hand that wasn't held, all the gifts never surrendered—and reap what you sow. The critics wind up condemned. The merciless fall and are not forgiven. The selfish wake up alone. The violent lie in pools of blood. Not all the time, and the price paid is not always quite so obvious. But these things certainly happen predictably enough to detect the pattern. You can recognize the sinful seeds by their fruit.

Tragically, however, there's more in view here than just the deserts that might come to us during our lifetimes. The verse above talked about *"destruction."* God's Word states that death, physical death that seals eternal separation from God, is the very thing sin insists on growing into. And while Sigmund Freud commented that "no one really believes in his own death," disbelieving won't keep you from dying anymore than denying gravity can help you when you're falling.

A nagging conscience does not just make stuff up. Sin is what it is nagging *about.* For a blunt biblical definition, "sin is lawlessness."[171] Sin means neither following the good will of God nor even wanting to. To use the Bible's own pictures, sin is failing to hit the target of goodness, it is willfully wandering from the right path and it is being bad enough to step across a good line. Sin is a hard heart, a stiff neck, a beast crouching at the door. We don't merely break commandments; something ugly stirs within that breaking. We declare our insane independence from God, our life; we

show him that we don't need him, don't want him, and are
not going to follow him anymore. Thus sin is irrational.
Though it makes a certain kind of sense to the sinner, sin is
ultimately self-destructive. Our very natures are filled up
with deep hostility, rebellion, pride, and selfish desire,
therefore, every human endeavor is tragically flawed from
the start.

It sticks in my ear, the ominous sound of the Hebrew
words *tohoo vavohoo,* which mean "formless and void."
These ancient words of Genesis describe the chaos at the
beginning of time before God began his ordering words,
"Let there be light." Significantly, this phrase is used one
other time in the Old Testament. God intoned through the
prophet Jeremiah *"tohoo vavohoo"* about the sinful condition
of the world[172] . . . as if human sin had ushered back in a kind
of deathly chaos, a sickening spiritual entropy.

It's the nature of the beast that we, being the sinners in
question, don't detect anything quite as bad as all that.
Ultimately, sin isn't measured by how *we* happen to feel
about it. Sin gets its gravity not only from its inherent badness but also from the infinite greatness of the one it
offends. Guilt looms precisely as large as the One who says,
"Do not," yet we do. Even "little" sins are a "big deal"
because God is. Sin is the history-long tragedy of
humankind's hostility toward God. Can't you tell that
something happened?

You see, humanity itself is implicated in a terrible primal
crime. Humankind has "a past." Spiritual death came to
our first parents when they sinned the *original* sin, when
they met with God face-to-face in the Garden of Eden and
slapped the original slap. And what happened to them also
happened to us, hiding, as we were, in their bodies.
Indeed, the human race, as one thing in Adam and Eve, fell
away from God when it rebelled against him. The very
skies seemed to crack like a mirror. The great human ship

ran aground. A once beautiful world just fell apart in certain ways, and we are living in the wreckage, daily stumbling through sin's consequences. That is to say, we aren't in the garden anymore. We live "East of Eden," where we hear the screams of childbirth and feel thorns tearing at our ankles.

So you may call sin the great No Wonder. It is not a pleasant thing to confront, but at least we have a perfectly consistent explanation for the way things are. No wonder it's so hard to keep a family together, make life work out to ten minutes of pristine happiness, or change ourselves in even little ways. Sin is the reason. Existence itself, as we now know it, is out of sync with its good Creator. *There's something wrong, terribly wrong, with everything.* Please don't say you hadn't noticed.

Cornelius Plantinga's chilling book *Not the Way It's Supposed to Be: A Breviary of Sin* deals with that pregnant Hebrew word *shalom*. The word is translated "peace," but "everything the way it's supposed to be" comes a little closer to the meaning. Shalom is unspoiled harmony with yourself and with every sister and brother, with the whole universe, and with God from whom, for whom, and to whom are all things. And everyone gets loved. And no one dies. Shalom is perfect well being, such as you've never seen but privately ache for. I'm supposed to sing every morning a song that won't be quiet. And you're supposed to laugh every day from a full, full heart. We're supposed to explore in perpetual discovery the landscape called his and stand together, beside ourselves, by some lake, on some green hill, in our sanctuary the size of the world, and robustly holler his name. *The way it's supposed to be.*

I think of that shalom . . . and I step disgusted away from my own cowardice and meanness and deliberate, blissful ignorance of human need. I let awaken my sense of sin. Yes, *sin.* I say the embarrassing word out loud, because loving

Jesus means being willing to use his words. The title of Plantinga's book is not a bad working definition of sin: "Not the way it's supposed to be."

There is something terribly wrong *with me!* Dear reader, don't think I'm talking (or writing) down to you. The truth is, I know why you sin. *I know.* Each of us is an intimate part of what's wrong with everything. I cannot sit high above the world I criticize and not get splashed myself.

Only Jesus can criticize and not get splashed. Think of his gentle healings, his patient teachings, his bold confrontations, his persistent forgiveness. Think of all his words: "What God has joined together, let no one separate!" and "Let the little children come to me!" and *"Little girl, get up!"* See how his whole life sparkled with *the way things were supposed to be.*

No such thing as sin? In our own popular culture are hints of the things most of us really believe. How many novels fairly weep over that something that is wrong with everything? How many of our favorite films take their power from that vague modern hunger *for redemption?* In *The Green Mile,* for just one example, a black mountain of a man, a condemned man of perpetual tears, is cursed to always feel within himself the ethical horrors of the human race, like bits of glass grinding in his brain. He sees in his mind the vile act another man commits and murmurs, "It's like that all over the world." He looks deep into the soul of a woman wasted by a foul disease and whispers the stirring, hopeful thing, "I see it." He sees what's really wrong and is one who can reach for it and perform the awful miracle of taking the horrible stuff into himself. In the end, the miracle worker dies, blameless but blamed, in the place of the guilty. We walk out of movies like that thoughtfully, with a dull ache behind our eyes. But I have a story twice better. In my story of redemption, the hero returns alive. Oh, and mine is true.

"Look, the Lamb of God, who takes away the sin of the world!"[173]

His incarnation was a quiet echo of the ancient "Let there be light." It is Christ who saw to the depth of you and me; it was sin that met his eyes. There was only one thing that would matter at all: his beautiful life given in exchange for ours, such as we were. Look at your own spiritual condition and be appalled; it is at this point that Christianity begins to speak its two languages of *sin* and *grace*. To hear the one is to be able, for the first time, to know the other. The paradox, as described by Paul Tournier, is that those who are most severe with themselves, calling sin by its name, are those who live in the most serene confidence in the mercy of God.

Awareness of sin and awareness of our Savior grow side by side.

Christianity has always measured the weight of humankind's actual guilt by the price that was required to atone for it. The very coming of Christ into the world can only mean that we were lost in the sight of God. The agony of God himself on Calvary and the urgency of the call to unite ourselves to him in faith tell us that the main human trouble was desperately difficult to fix, even for Divinity, and that sin is the longest-running of human emergencies. But don't be afraid. If sin is the ugly man-made scratches on the human shore, grace is the smoothing, covering tide. The news is good.

God has taken away your sin.

Because you are loved and because you are grateful, you mumble attempts at encouragement and fumble with small acts of kindness—new seeds you sow in hopes of what they will become.

As for me, I survey the faces of my loved ones and I see that the law of the farm has from time to time, more often than not, been set aside for me. In their presence and their kindness, I am reaping more than I have ever sown, grace upon grace.

The painting at the Christian bookstore holds me in its grip.

It is a portrait of the face of Christ, yet his face is partially obscured by the person he embraces, by an anonymous head that is turned away and covered by a cloth.

The fierceness of that hug. The warmth of that smile. The shine in his eyes . . . so happy. So happy. Yet a hint of the pain behind his costly joy remains in Jesus' face. And with his loved one's head all covered up like that . . . it could be anyone at all.

The longing for what this picture contains wakes up, sudden and unexpectedly intense. It matches the depth of human desire for the *Agnus Dei*. The Lamb of God. The *Sar Shalom*.

That is, the Prince of everything the way it's supposed to be.

"I don't care for organized religion"

Judas chose to go it alone. He worked out his questions and did battle with his personal demons all by himself. He walked out of the upper room, made his escape down the back stairs, and the Twelve became the Eleven. Now, in all outward appearance, everything with Judas was fine. When he left that evening, the other disciples were willing to see good reason for his absence—he was probably out doing something for the poor he always talked about. But make no mistake. Walking away from that circle of Jesus' followers, such as they were, meant walking away from Jesus himself.

And when grief came to Judas, when it gathered up its full man-crushing weight, he sought people who might help him carry it or who might help him somehow fix the mess he had made or who at least might tell him it was going to be all right. Everyone needs someone to talk to, even Judas.

So he confessed his sin, making a gut-wrenching admission—"I have betrayed innocent blood!" —to the wrong sort of people. The so-called spiritual leaders of Israel didn't know Jesus, therefore, they didn't know grace. "Judas, there is forgiveness for you" and "there is one who loves you still" were not things they knew how to say. With the shrug of their shoulders and their "What is that to us?" these spiritual leaders, in affect, just killed him.

I can't help but think: "If only . . ."

If only Judas had stayed in the upper room. There was always a place for him there, regardless of the secrets he hid in his heart. If only he had examined his own heart in the presence of the One who always knew what to say. In the real reasons Judas wanted to leave that little church— his greed, his anger, his pride—he could have seen precisely the reason he needed to stay.

Judas needed forgiveness. It proved to be the one thing he couldn't live without. And there in that upper room was forgiveness personified, for there was Christ holding together John, the one who leaned on his right side.

On Jesus' other side was an empty place.

(Please read John 13:18-30 and Matthew 27:1-10.)

Having spent many years in Christian leadership, this joke still brings a smile to my face. One day someone said, "I don't go for organized religion."

Someone else answered, "It's not *that* organized!"

However, the real question people are asking is, How can something as personal as religious faith depend in any significant way on institutionalized religion? They get more out of a contemplative walk alone in the woods, so they say, than from an hour of corporate worship. I too embrace the natural beauty of God's world and crave the solitude of a quiet lake. When the setting sun creates a dazzling golden path across the rippling water directly toward me on my pier, my soul stands up to see. I really feel as if I could walk that ethereal road directly into heaven, *into him.*

Of course, I cannot.

Although there are things that can be learned about God in nature—so awesome, so extravagant—the thing we most need to know about him does not rustle in the leaves or shimmer on the waves. And we do not figure it out all by ourselves. The thing we need to know is, How does he—so above and so beyond—come down to us?

I must explain that while religious faith can be called personal in many respects, in its truest sense it is not. Christianity is *not* personal if by *personal* you mean that the Christian faith is something we find within our deepest selves or is something we work out individually, privately, or internally.

The Christian is one who no longer seeks such things as salvation, peace, or hope within him or herself—in the end only darkness and death come from within. The Christian looks outside of him or herself and finds every good thing in Jesus Christ as the Word of God brings him near. As Dietrich Bonhoeffer pointed out, the Christian lives wholly by that external Word, not by his or her own personal feelings. That is, the Word comes to the sinner from outside of him or her, *declaring* the sinner guilty even when he or she doesn't *feel* guilty and *declaring the sinner forgiven even when he or she doesn't feel forgiven.*[174]

"Whenever our hearts condemn us . . . God is greater than our hearts."[175]

The Christian is one who daily hungers and thirsts for the righteousness and who constantly desires the absolution—the "I have loved you and have forgiven you now and forever"—that are in Christ. These things are found in only one place in this entire groaning world, namely, in God's redeeming Word.

"For a brief moment I abandoned you, but with deep compassion I will bring you back."[176]

We taste that sweet redemption in the bread and wine that are, respectively, Christ's body and blood "given *for you.*"[177] This redemption also comes connected to the baptismal water on the strength of God's promise: "Baptized *into Christ*."[178] The Word and sacraments are God's things. They are found precisely where he himself has put them, in the center of every true gathering of believers in Christ. Their presence is the one true mark of the church and of the company God keeps among his people. When we can't raise ourselves up to him on the ladder of religious feelings, he comes all the way down to us through these means. It is receiving this Good News again and again that keeps believing individuals repentant and alive to God. It is learning to draw always more deeply from the well of salvation that means we are growing up into Christ.

In the same way, the church itself, that body of all people who believe in Jesus, cannot continue to be his church for one solitary day without the fresh supply of grace that comes from him through the gospel, that is, without the novel thing he does for believers' faith with each Word of his that strikes their ears. Christians praise a God whose tender mercies arrive "new every morning."[179] And the whole thing doesn't come down to how "organized" they are, thank God.

A sad memory of mine is the day I sat with a couple who hadn't been in church to receive that grace for over five years. They tried to assure me: "Pastor, don't worry about us. We still believe in God. And we're doing everything we can to be good people so we can go to heaven." They are certainly not Judases, betraying Jesus outright. But are they Christians? I honestly don't know. I only know that there is no spiritual life in their words whatsoever. Not even close.

Here's what I constantly find: The assurance of peace with God becomes a very weak thing when I try to work it up within myself. But Christ is strong in the Word of God that comes through a brother or a sister. He designed Christian life in just this way: we need one another, we belong together. For God has put reconciliation in the mouths of the "two or three" who gather in Jesus' name, who meet one another as bearers of salvation. *"There am I,"* Jesus told us, *"with them."*

Why then would anyone *want* to be an isolated, separated Christian? As Fredrick Buechner put it, there is an "Us-ness" to the Christian faith. Those who belong to Christ by faith also belong to one another, like parts of a human body that are perfectly fitted together. Does a hand, a mouth, or even a little toe strike out on its own? Regardless of the part you are meant to play among the believers—to encourage the hurting, to teach the little ones, to serve the needy—if you don't play it, if you aren't there, you are missed.

If you are a member of Christ's body by faith, then there is meaning for you in taking your place in service to his body, the church. The important thing to point out is in how many respects we cannot possibly express by ourselves all that it means to be a Christian.

"Where two or three come together in my name, there am I with them."[180] That's what Jesus said, and the context is especially important. This lovely promise sparkles in the midst of Jesus' longest extended discourse about *forgiveness.* Before this verse is the principle to follow "if your brother sins against you," and immediately after this verse is Peter's classic question, "How many times shall I forgive?" This context indicates to me that the "two or three" Jesus has in mind don't merely meet to chat over coffee or to arrange a play date for their kids. They "come together" when one has been bruised by another, when someone has been hurt and is angry, when the two or three have just fallen apart and something ugly has come between them . . . then the golden opportunity arrives.

We find out what it means to belong to Christ and what it means to be the church.

Please think about it. How will you learn to forgive your brother or love your sister *all by yourself*? How will you learn humility, patience, or anything that can be called gracious *all by yourself?* These are the things that do not even come into play until we're together . . . and someone has offended someone . . . and someone says, "I forgive you" . . . and some two or three who had been separated in their mere humanness come together again.

Then we breathe the unmistakable fragrance of Christ.

Two deeply cherished members of my congregation were angry. They were hurt. They were leaving our Christian family for good, and there was nothing anyone could say. A woman saw their grief as they stood in the lobby of our church, perhaps for the last time.

What happened next they would still wonder about and talk about years later.

This woman ached for them and felt compelled to walk over to them and to say . . . God knows what. She hardly remembers what it was, only that it rose up from the Scripture she hides in her heart.

They can only report that their anger, stored away for months, just lifted. The hurt they had held so long was simply gone, replaced by peace and warmth . . . and something More that they still can't quite explain. Perhaps I can.

"Where two or three come together in my name . . .

"There am I."

"Can a loving God send people to hell?"

What kind of man is this, with what kind of heart?

Jesus tells his friends how much he has longed for this last Passover supper with them . . . knowing full well what comes after it. With candlelight dancing in his eyes, he surveys a table set with bread and wine, bitters and roasted lamb. Everything has been prepared.

From the available evidence, we can reconstruct at least a partial seating arrangement of the 13 men who gathered around that low wooden table. We find Judas reclining on cushions to Jesus' immediate left—the place reserved for the intimate friend. There is no distance between them; they even dip their bread into the same sauce dish. This closeness explains the things spoken in the upper room that not all the disciples seem to hear. Not all are privy to the dreadful secrets passing between Jesus and Judas.

"What you are about to do, do quickly."[181]

The relationship between Jesus and Judas holds moments of warmth—Jesus caresses Judas' feet in his two hands and washes them—moments of foreshadowing—"you will not always have me"—and moments of complete and awful understanding—"One of you will betray me." Always,

always, the Betrayed reaches for the betrayer, even in the moment of the treachery itself later in the garden. Judas pulls himself away from Jesus and from that famous kiss to hear a word designed to reach out to him and slap him awake: "Friend!"

"Friend, do what you came for."

What more can Jesus do? There is one last thing . . . in only a few more hours.

No matter how many times I read the story, it always goes the same. Jesus loves Judas. Judas betrays Jesus. Jesus offers his life for Judas. Judas throws his life away. If Judas thought suicide would make his pain go away, the Bible is far too clear on this point.

His pain is just getting warmed up.

And I ask you to consider in the story of Jesus and Judas, who abandons whom? Just who gives up on whom? You want to ask, "How can a loving God send people to hell?" But scan the record again. It doesn't read like a story of a man being sent anywhere. It's the story of a man rejecting every possible good, going his own way and destining himself for the dark. Do you see?

The only one trying to stand in his way *is the Son of God.*

(Please read Matthew chapters 26 and 27.)

How could a loving God send people to hell? First of all, thank you for treating the matter of eternity as if it has some relevance. It does. As I write this chapter, the nation is reeling from the destruction by terrorists of the Twin Towers in New York City. The terrorists, Muslim fundamentalists, certainly had no remorse, no last second, "Lord, what have we done?" Just seconds before their suicide attack killed thousands of people and devastated thousands of families, they were very likely smiling, maybe even laughing, quite possibly cheering. What about a few seconds *after?* Were they laughing still? or perhaps living in blissful nonexistence? Is that how their stories end? In other words, *did they get away with it?* Does that sound right to you? Me neither.

You ask, "How can a good God send people to hell?" I ask, "How could a just God tolerate the evil we see in this world?" I think of such things as are said to children, such things as are done to women . . . and I want God to care and want God to be outraged. I want God to remember. I can't imagine that God, especially our good God, wouldn't care about the way we are living and the things people do to people.

Fine. You're with me so far. But hell? My mind too recoils at the thought of an eternal hell for sinners who never repent. Yet I have to ask whether *it* is to be trusted, that is, this emotional, knee-jerk reaction of a *sinner* on the topic of what should happen to sinners. Jesus himself—who is, in a gross understatement, to ethics what Einstein is to physics and Michael Jordan is to basketball—saw no problem with the doctrine of hell. Far from it. His life and teachings are incomprehensible apart from the real and awful danger he saw looming in the afterlife for human beings. The ethically brilliant Christ saw clearly the necessity of hell. Do I understand justice better than Jesus? Am I the judge of God?

If you argue against the existence of two eternities—one with God forever and the other without him—if you argue against the patient justice of the one who made us, you are arguing for the utter meaninglessness of all things. You are arguing that finally nothing we do in life matters at all and that you and I, and Judas and Jesus—every pang of every conscience to the contrary—play meaningless games with nothing really at stake.

I'll admit, it's difficult even to think about the first moment a soul spends in hell, what the realization that *it will never end* must be like. But what I cannot at all evict from my mind is the knowledge that our human sense of justice is the echo of something larger than us. For in all the judgments we persist in making—even those that judge judging itself—and in all the stamping of our tiny feet, we speak as if we think we're saying something true. And we are. For it is written across the cosmos that some things are wrong, dreadfully and unspeakably wrong. There is such a thing as divine, perfect wrath—a necessary corollary of divine goodness. There is a God in heaven whose very nature is, as the Holy One, to oppose every evil with all that he is and to respond with awful justice. Would you ask God not to be God? Have you mistaken his patience regarding the state the world is in for moral apathy? That is a miscalculation. God's immutable righteousness is just one thing we need to see when we stumble at the question of hell.

Next, we need to see ourselves. Do not get the idea that hell is a reality only for the Osama bin Ladens of the world. We need to think again about the distinction we try to draw between the "really bad people" and ourselves. We need to take a deeper look into the nature of our own sin. There is plenty of badness within us.

Deep down we like to think of ourselves as strugglers— "if anyone knew what I go through, they wouldn't blame me for the things I do." A little wound is all we need to justify any thought or any act. Yet in our own private shames and personal vices, we see that same damning quality as is found in the worst things humans have done. Surely, when people reject God—*reject God!*—it is more serious than words can say, and God cannot be blamed for leaving them to the natural consequences of that rejection.

But you see, this is the nature of *every* sin, even the very smallest act in which we do what the God of our existence says we must *not*. All sin is a rejection of God himself, an act of insane defiance, and a basic denial of his goodness.

Human iniquity is a desperate and feverish sawing on the very branch we sit on. I see in my own unlovely life something in me that is always saying to God: "Leave me alone. I don't need you. I don't want you. Don't tell me how I should be. I don't belong to you."

And because I discover that meaning in my own sin, I couldn't hold it against him if I were to go to hell, if after a lifetime of sun and rain, endless grace and endless chances, he should say: "All right then. Have it your way. I leave you alone." This, expressed in the dark and in the fire, is hell. It doesn't come for those who merely fail to believe the right things. Hell is what sin and sinners deserve. It is the right place for God to send those who despise the One they know is real by creation and through their own conscience. They know. The consequences are somehow even worse for those who have heard and have refused the call of Christ. In the words of C. S. Lewis, people get to hell *"on their own steam."* To reject God's good and holy will, *then* reject his free salvation, *then* reject his right to condemn the contemptible or to be God at all . . . well, what is he to do? Hell is filled with people who still want nothing to do with him. In fact, God did not create hell in the sense of making something new. He merely removes his love and all his life-giving blessings. What is left for the damned to experience, God's unending wrath that punishes every sin—this is hell's essence.

Someone observed that when a fig tree outside Jerusalem withered away, it was not because of something Jesus did but because of something he *stopped* doing. He stopped sustaining, holding, looking on in silent benediction. And the fig tree withered away. So it is for the soul in hell—the one that didn't want to be disturbed—when God finally, fully withdraws his love and blessings.

If we were not sinners ourselves, if thinking itself had not been damaged in the fall, we would see all of these things completely. In fact, the Scriptures do not only say that justice will be accomplished at the end of the world but also that justice will be seen to be done, so that every mouth will be shut.[182]

I take no pleasure in this chapter, but I cannot apologize for echoing the message of Christ: *Meet me as Savior or prepare to meet me as Judge.* Hell is not a doctrine gleefully pronounced on other people over whom I feel morally superior. I also deserve to go to hell because of all my sin. This is not something I want to be true, but Christian beliefs, unlike so many others, aren't formed by mere preference. More than anything else, what keeps this one awful thing on the list of all the beautiful things I believe through Christ . . . is Christ. I fear that if you deny hell because you don't like to think about it (a luxury Jesus didn't have), you can never really see him. Until you see that something in you saying, "Leave me alone," you catch no glimpse of that something in him saying, "Over my dead body. I won't let you go." Deny hell and you can never see very far into the heart of Christ, who walked up a hill under a threatening sky and called your disaster on himself. Deny hell and nothing Jesus did will make any sense. Especially, you will miss how intense, how passionate, how personal everything is that we read in his deeds and in his face those final hours. The message of his anguish is meant for you: "I don't want you to go to hell! I don't want you to go to hell! *I won't let you go to hell!*"

Just what did you think his crucifixion was for?

I don't write of hell to keep you afraid. The dominant note is not fear but unspeakable relief, gratitude that takes your breath away, to think of the horror you never need to know and what it cost for you to be rescued. I write so that you might be bonded to Christ, inseparably connected to him forever. You must go deeper than your sentimental thoughts of Jesus as your best friend and kindly helper in tough times. He is those things. But meet him first as

Rescuer. Deliverer. I want you to experience that walk toward heaven that begins just outside the gates of hell, where he walked through fire for you. All I want is for you to never, never forget what he did for you.

All God asks is that you let a little of the sorrow in—the sorrow about your own life—and that you trust the One who died for you. Then Jesus will come at last and gather you to your home, where you will always have him.

When we talk about the tragedy of hell, it's important to keep the story of Judas in the front. It's one time we get to see the look on God's face as the unthinkable happens. He reaches for someone. His hand comes back empty. Sorrow opens up at his feet. This is the betrayal, the disbelief, the devastation that is Jesus in the Garden of Gethsemane. Jesus looks at his betrayer and calls him friend . . . as Judas wrestles himself away.

"People are basically good"

The Sanhedrin, the ruling council of the Jews, wanted Jesus murdered in the worst way. Jesus made the Jewish rulers look bad. Pontius Pilate declared Jesus an innocent man before satiating the rulers' hunger for an execution—to keep them happy.

So it was that first century Israel and first century Rome—crowning human achievements in ethics and morality, politics and law—conspired in humanity's gravest atrocity. Witness the crucifixion of Christ, who had never done any harm, who only healed, only helped, only loved. His only crime was speaking the truth. But don't lose any sleep over what the people of Israel and Rome did, our brightest and our best.

"People are basically good."

So please excuse Judas Iscariot. When he surrendered his teacher to hellish agony, he was a confused and complicated man. Peter was under a lot of strain when he denied even knowing his truest friend's name. Soldiers only followed orders when they stripped the world's best man, flogged him, beat him, tortured him, ridiculed him, and nailed his flesh and bones onto the boards. Don't be too tough on the ordinary folks who clamored for these things—this was an isolated incident in their otherwise

decent lives. So their leaders were laughing a little bit. Don't let it trouble you. No need to challenge your moral ambiguity or let a little thing like reality shake up your view of human nature. It was everything these people did or said or thought or felt that was bad. Not them.
People are basically good.
(Please read Luke chapters 22 and 23.)

I know of a psychologist who customarily asks new patients this question: What is it about yourself that you are least willing to share with other people? The two most common answers he hears are: "I feel utterly worthless" and "I don't love anyone as I should." Naturally, he considers it his primary task to contradict them. I'm not so sure.

There is nothing so bad that we Christians won't say it about ourselves, that is, who we are by birth and who we would remain if God left us to ourselves.

"I know that nothing good lives in me, that is, in my sinful nature."[183]

You wonder how we can say such things. I wonder how you can deny such things in the light of such humanly authored disasters as the one we call 9-11. The successful terrorist attack involved a thing so awful it never even entered our minds: the diabolical conversion of passenger airliners, filled to human capacity, into guided missiles. These slammed into the fragile lives of thousands of innocent bystanders. All around the world people clapped at the thought that finally we Americans would *know*. We would know what the world is really like. But how could it have happened? Journalist Tom Friedman makes a compelling point that the failure on the part of America was not so much a failure of our intelligence services or national security, foreign policy or immigration law.

It was a *"failure of the imagination."*

We had failed to imagine the depth of human hatred. We did not fully plumb the evil of human intentions or conceive in advance the inhuman brutality of the act. Because people are basically good. Everyone knows this.

If I work now to shake off that blind faith in the inherent goodness of humanity—for it is blind to history, to psychology, and to the truth hiding in our own worst moments of the last few days—part of that shaking comes from observing humanity *at its worst.*

This particular objection to our faith—people are basically good—had more wind in its sails before 1945. What happened in 1945? Auschwitz. Bergen-Belzen. Piles of gold fillings and women's hair. Photographs of emaciated bodies stacked like cordwood rocked the optimistic view of humankind to its very core. These were things about which we vowed "never again." Should we now try to forget? Should we determine not to see the evil that ordinary human beings are capable of, from the millions starved at the whim of greedy third-world bureaucrats to the millions upon millions murdered on the empty altar of communism? Were these events aberrations on the human landscape?

Or were they horrifying epiphanies? Were the thousands upon thousands of people involved somehow of a different category than the rest of us or made of different stuff? Someone has said, "In an avalanche, every snowflake pleads not guilty" . . . but does that really work? Is the cowardice of individuals exonerated by the fact that they were merely swept along in the cascade of human events?

Though you and I have not been party to such overt evils as those I've just mentioned, the disturbing truth is that we have each done *the evil we are capable of.* I may be no Hitler. But do I really get credit for not being as evil as Hitler if I have avoided some outward expression of evil simply because I was too timid or not talented enough? if I didn't have the same opportunity as someone else or was fearful of the consequences to my life or to my conscience? I have done the evil that was within my reach. I have made my wife cry. I have betrayed my friend's trust. I have thought thoughts that would kill me if you knew them.

We must not evade the real question: Just where does evil come from in the first place? Where does it originate? The answer is the worst possible news from the best possible Man: *"For out of the heart come evil thoughts, murder, adultery, sexual immorality, theft, false testimony, slander."*[184]

Evil comes from the heart, which is to say, from an inexhaustible supply. It comes *from us*. Where else? In his novel *The Hobbit*, J. R. R. Tolkien commented, "It does not do to leave a dragon out of your calculations, if you live near him." The dragon is human evil. On a large scale, think of what has happened to every human attempt at a utopian society built on naïve ideas about human nature. Disaster. On a more personal scale, think of what happens in an intimate relationship when people are unable to repent and when forgiveness—the inevitable need—is given no room. The intimacy just dies. The result has always been disillusionment, cynicism, and heartache when human selfishness and prideful competition were not taken into account.

Perhaps an analogy will help. Consider a watch, expensive and pretty, that just doesn't happen to tell time correctly. Would you consider it a "basically good" watch anyway? I doubt it. How "good" it is must be measured according to its purpose. The watch may have many pleasing aspects in its design and appearance, all of which carry a certain promise of what it might have been . . . yet the watch, *as a watch*, is worthless. Once we realize that worship and selfless love are to us what telling time is to watches—the very things we are *for*—we can hardly call ourselves basically good when every inclination is leaning the other way. Our inborn hatred of God is aroused as soon as we find out from his Word who he really is and what he really wants of us.

I should add that I personally like people a great deal. As with the broken watch, you can still detect in broken, fallen people the mastery of their original design, the capacity for relationship and beauty that the Maker intended. The pleasing aspects of surface personality whisper in heartbreaking times about what might have been if we really were as good as we tried so desperately to appear. Indeed, if our private thoughts were all broadcast out loud, I think you know this chapter would not need to be written.

Earlier I asked you to consider humanity at its worst. Now think about us *at our best*. Even the best of human love is more clearly seen as the consuming desire to *be* loved. Human love is a hunger to *have* not to *give*, which is to say it is not love at all in the highest sense. The drive of one person to find another is powerful and the satisfactions of human connection are intense. Take a mother and her newborn child. Her heart is full with the euphoria of a relationship in which every human boundary seems to have fallen. The mother is so needed and so accepted. But what is a mother capable of when this need is no longer being met? A woman sends a car full of her children to the bottom of a lake. The horror is that she looks just like one of us. . . . She is.

But "people are basically good."

You see, the dragon inevitably wakes up in miserable self-absorption that excludes real happiness, anger that destroys relationships, and pride that turns worship into a self-flattering sham. For we are, by nature, worthless.

Now make it personal. Where, really, should my thoughts run if I want to know what sort of person I am and of what quality? Should I think of myself at my best, the person acting well in pleasant circumstances? Is that who I really am? Or must I shudder to remember myself at my worst, when pressures and problems conspired to reveal me to me? Which is real, my well-crafted public persona or my private ugliness? Which colors are my true ones? *Do I love anyone as I should?*

I suppose the way to avoid seeing the badness within us is to concede it might be true for those who think that way or to say that there is no such thing as morality so as to distinguish real good from bad. But the cost of moral ambiguity is too high. If we have no ear for the wrong notes in the human song and no longer wince at the discordant noise, then we cannot discern the right notes in our music or in anyone else's.

Don't you see? The woman who tells you there is no such thing as truth is really telling you not to believe what she says, because she doesn't believe it herself. The man who tells you there is no such thing as morality is only telling you that he is not to be trusted with anything tender you care about, or with anyone, because he holds himself to no standard higher than himself. The people who say there is no such thing as God are telling you that they are their own gods, though they are not qualified for the job. Those who reject the concept of guilt as too inhibiting or destructive are only telling you that they are not willing to feel within themselves the pain they cause others.

And those who say that "people are basically good" only admit that they never dare to look in the mirror. They admit that their company is not safe in the long run because their own shabbiest instincts remain alive and well and are not dealt with in any serious way.

The reason I take such pains to point to such awful truths, indeed, the reason I dare to distinguish "psychological need seeking satisfaction" from actual love is quite simple. *There is such a thing as love.*

Watch Jesus. Listen to him gasp out words like "Father, forgive them" as men sit on his chest and pound spikes through his wrists. Jesus alone fully saw the horrible nature present in humanity and sacrificed himself to it. When he was crushed, when he was broken, the fragrance of *who he is* was released. This is when he was best revealed. *"Father, forgive them."* To hear such words is to know that they are not of this world.

"Love comes from God . . . because God is love."[185]

When the holy wind blew around the gruesome hill, a Roman centurion and an outcast of the Jews saw such Good in Jesus they knew it could only be the mark of God. Here was a different kind of life, revealed in the great crushing.

Out of his heart proceeded forgiveness, mercy, goodness, compassion, truth . . .

I think I'm a pretty nice guy doing well . . . until I see him. Then I repent in the presence of one so good. Let him break our hearts and shine his light inside them. Let us admit that our need for God was not for a helping hand or a gentle nudge in the right direction. We needed him to save us. So he did. Beyond any explanation, we are worth something to him. And now . . . there is nothing so good we will not say it about Christ, who sees us as we are, who loves us and makes his home *within us.*

It would not have been his last word, the one that called you bad. But this did not occur to you. It was beyond your wildest dreams, a willing crucifixion by the very maker of iron and wood and men.

And you never thought he would rise.

It was wholly unforeseen that *his* kind of life, his resurrection life, would spark alive within you, leading you to repent and turn toward him. It was unforeseen what that turning was supposed to mean to you forever. "No mind has conceived what God has prepared for those who love him."[186]

If it should happen to you, that unnecessary disaster of losing God forever, it will not be a failure of his goodness or justice, not a failure of his mercy or of his love.

Call it a failure of the imagination.

The truth of the dying, rising Christ never entered your mind.

"Jesus is just one of many great men"

The day arrived for filming the crucifixion. The actor, Bruce Marchiano, daring to play the role of Jesus, staggered toward the vacant cross lying on the ground. But he stumbled in exhaustion and landed facedown in the stones a few feet shy of his mark. That wasn't planned. No longer on script, he looked over to the wood just out of reach and had a curious impulse. He lunged for it. And having achieved his goal, the cross, he tightly squeezed his eye closed and gripped it. Like a prize.

There's no reason to think that moment actually happened at Christ's crucifixion. Yet the *spirit* of it is true. Have you read the account of Jesus' final trek to Jerusalem? They were on the road as usual, he and his followers, but something was different. He wasn't holding back for stragglers. He was out in front. No child was held in his arms. He wasn't gently painting pictures of the kingdom of God for his followers. He was scaring them. "They were on their way up to Jerusalem, with Jesus leading the way, and the disciples were astonished, while those who followed were afraid."[187]

Look a little deeper, and see that the entire life of Christ was just this, a striding for Jerusalem, a

fast-walk toward a crucifixion. This is the God of the Scriptures running to my rescue. "I set my face like flint."[188]
What is the greatness of Jesus? This is first: He had compassion on me. My need reached him and was felt like a kick in the stomach. So he saved me.
(Please read Mark 10:32-34.)

What are we to make of Jesus Christ? C. S. Lewis pointed out that the real question is, What is he to make of us? A fly deciding what to make of an elephant is not without its comic elements. On a more serious note, Lewis made the observation that "if Jesus is false, he is of no importance. If he's true, he is of infinite importance. The one thing he can never be is moderately important." The truth is, it is Christ himself that is asking from the pages of the gospels: "What about you? Who do you say I am?"[189]

To reply that he is just one of many great men does not deal intelligently with the uniqueness of Christ jutting up from the whole vast landscape of human history. If you'll allow one more nod to the Oxford don C. S. Lewis, here is his take on Jesus: "You can shut him up for a fool, you can spit at him, and kill him as a demon; or you can fall at his feet and call him Lord and God. But let us not come with any patronizing nonsense about his being a great human teacher. He has not left that option open to us. He did not intend to."[190]

What does he mean by that? Once you say Jesus is not everything Christianity makes him out to be, you are obligated to provide an alternative explanation to the phenomenon that he is. It's not so easy. Once you say he is not Lord, you are compelled to support one of the following premises: he was both a great moral teacher *and* a disgusting liar for claiming to be God; he was both a great moral teacher *and* a raving lunatic for thinking he was God; he was a great moral teacher even though we *really* know almost nothing about him that isn't legendary . . . or I suppose you can feebly say he wasn't a great moral teacher at all. But how else shall I say this? None of these *work*.

For starters, Jesus Christ has been, on the strength of his teaching, the central figure in Western civilization for the past 20 centuries. During this time, the arts, education, medicine, science, justice, charity, and civil rights have all grown best out of Christian soil. These facts and the very depth and sanity of Jesus' words argue that he is *the* great moral teacher. And here's the rub: his scandalous claim of Deity is the inextricable, gravitational center of all his good teaching and of his very life. They asked him under oath, "Tell us if you are the Christ, the Son of God." He answered in the affirmative, with "Yes, it is as you say."[191]

The greatest teacher made the greatest claim. What will you do with it?

Was he *lying* when he claimed to be God? Is he a great moral teacher who asked obedient millions to lay down their lives for what he knew to be false? It is an unjustifiable contradiction that the man of such moral discernment, which has eclipsed that of every other human being, should be the author of such an utterly despicable fraud. And does a religious huckster of that magnitude change the world with the beauty of his character and ethic? Not only that, does a shyster take his lie all the way to a tortured death? Consider that those who know God best are the ones most profoundly aware of personal guilt. Yet the wise and gentle Jesus, who lived closer to God than any other person, lived free of any sense of any personal sin whatsoever.[192]

Then was he *deluded* in claiming to be God? Neither megalomaniacs nor psychotics are marked by humility, grace, and brilliance of thought; nor do they achieve the beautiful cohesiveness in life that millions wish to emulate; nor do others bloom and thrive in relationship with such people; nor do these people convince those that actually know them of their godlike qualities, especially not the likes of Saul of Tarsus. Saul was not only a positively brilliant man but also a man who did not *want* to be convinced. All this explains why it is virtually unheard of for even the most voracious critics of Christianity to actually take on Christ himself. No one dares make the case that he was either a shady or an unstable character.

Perhaps the man himself is the stuff of *legend*. Do you realize that if we didn't have the New Testament, we could still learn all the basic biographical information about Jesus from unimpeachable, unbiased first century voices, such as a Jewish historian named Josephus and Roman historians named Pliny and Tacitus to name just a few? In fact, 39 ancient sources corroborate over one hundred facts about Jesus Christ.[193] (As reported separately by Phlegon and Thallus, there is fascinating circumstantial evidence as well, such as the earthquake and an impossibly broad eclipse that coincides with the death of Christ.) Besides, is it silly, superstitious legend that, in the words of historian Philip Schaff, "This Jesus . . . without money or arms conquered more millions than Alexander, Caesar, Muhammad and Napoleon"?[194] It seems absurd to suggest that such a wake in the ocean of world history was left behind *by nothing!*

Were the words of Christ that lay claim to equality with God and the miracle of Jesus stepping alive out of his own death later legendary revisions? So then the disciples were utterly changed from cowering cynics to loud, smiling martyrs *by nothing?* Or was "that social earthquake" whereby, in the space of those few short years in question, thousands of Jewish people altered their most fundamental traditions and beliefs caused by nothing? Thousands of Jewish people abandoned their Sabbath Day restrictions, mandatory cir-

cumcision, and animal sacrifice, their separation from Gen-
tiles, and their fond political hopes for a Messiah. These
beliefs and traditions had made their lives meaningful and
had identified their people for centuries. However, they now
found clear justification for each of these dizzying changes
in their own ancient Scriptures.

It won't weaken my case to admit that there are a few
precedents for legendary material attaching to historic fig-
ures, for example, the Buddha. But the comparison to
Christ is weak. Whereas legend, by the very nature of
things, only develops after centuries (and all contemporary
witnesses) have passed, the historical attestation of Jesus'
words and deeds by countless credible witnesses dates back
to *his own generation*. (By the way, Buddha lived in the
sixth century B.C, and his life was recorded in the first century A.D.)

When the apostle Paul writes, "What I received I passed
on to you as of first importance,"[195] he refers to his meeting
with the other apostles shortly after the saving events in
Jerusalem. He then records the creedal statements he
received there—see them for yourself in 1 Corinthians chapter 15. (See also Philippians chapter 2 and 1 Timothy chapter 3 to name a couple similar places). Thus we have the
testimony of the church's convictions about Jesus that were
*fully formed within two to five years of the earth-shattering
events themselves*. It's all there. He died for our sins. He was
buried. He was raised.

Church historian Jaroslav Pelikan demonstrates that the
oldest Christian sermons, the oldest accounts of a Christian
martyr, the oldest pagan reports of the church, and the oldest liturgical prayers all refer to Jesus as Lord and God.
Scholar Gary Habermas identifies seven secular sources and
several early creeds that establish the deity of Christ as "def-
initely present in the earliest church."[196] There is nothing
comparable in all recorded history for a legend developing

so loudly, so uniformly, so publicly, so free of the flavor of mythical embellishment, and above all, so very, very close to the events themselves. Ready for a bottom line? Unless the disciples of Jesus, though willing to die for him, completely forgot who Jesus actually was or had no hand in the forming of the church's beliefs, the idea that Jesus was a legend makes no sense, not to those who care about history.

Philip Schaff concluded: "A character so original, so complete, so uniformly consistent, so perfect, so human and yet so high above all human greatness, can be neither a fraud nor a fiction. . . . *It would take more than a Jesus to invent a Jesus.*"[197] That is to say, there's no one like the Lord Christ. He is unparalleled, unduplicatable, unconcoctable.

Who do *you* say he is? The option left to you, of course, is that our uninventable Jesus is everything he claimed to be, everything true Christians believe. If you're *still* not convinced, consider a fascinating, backdoor approach to the question of Christ: the Great Proposition from Josh McDowell. If God chose to become a man, what would he be like? Ever think of that? It's a very good question. I mean, how could God with skin on let us know it was really him?

Well, he could prophesy his coming centuries in advance and in fingerprint-like detail so that his arrival would be unmistakable. If God became a man, he would be certain to have an utterly unique birth as his entrance into human history. You could expect an outbreak of miracles like signposts pointing to him and to what you could expect would be a life lived more beautifully, more perfectly than any other human life. His words would be the greatest ever spoken—with lasting, universal influence—and he, the mightiest factor in world history, would make sure those words would reach to the ends of earth and of time. And not only would Immanuel—"God with us"—satisfy the spiritual hunger in humanity but he would somehow overcome humanity's most pervasive and feared enemy. He would come to do something about death. Does any of this sound familiar? This is Jesus Christ and only Jesus Christ.

But enough of reasoned, historical arguments. I promise I'll stop piling them up if you promise to stop fending them off. The reason I bother with them at all is to discredit the *un*reasoned, *un*historical potshots at Christ—and this is my heart—wishing only that you might stand face-to-face with the thing itself, with God loving you, a sinner, in Christ; that I might leave you with him and his mercy; that you might ponder alone for a moment the legitimate scandal that remains, the cross itself—"that God was reconciling the world to himself in Christ."[198]

If anything is going to persuade you that this is true, it's the words themselves. It is the Word of God, by the power of his Spirit, that works more than intellectual assent. It crushes your heart on the matter of all your sin. Four or five of his words—"Your sins are forgiven" or "Yes, I am coming soon"—can do more for you than any human attempt to justify them. By God's power alone, the last two words of "Jesus died *for me*" jump the gap between head and heart. The great Lord Christ issues his mighty commands.

"Repent . . . that times of refreshing may come."[199]

"Trust in God; trust also in me."[200]

"Do not be afraid."

These are the grace imperatives—these words hold within them the power to accomplish in you the very things they command. It's not unlike the time Jesus told the little dead girl to get up and live. So she did.

We were sitting down to eat in a family restaurant. My little redhead, Hannah, flashed the world's most contagious smile to a woman sitting in the next booth. The woman did a most amazing thing. She didn't smile back. I didn't know such a thing was even possible.

The sudden, unexpected, undeserved way in which God smiled at this world in Christ—the light of the knowledge of the glory of God all in one beaming human face—ought to fill the vast, unthinkable spaces in the universe with shouts of "Glory! Halleluiah!" God has given us his Son. Are you going to go on saying he didn't? Or will you smile back?

This is the issue. Who is Jesus? What do *you* say?

"People don't really change"

The fathers killed the prophets. With ruthless efficiency, the sons killed the Christ. People don't change.

But . . . but that story Jesus told . . . do you remember it?

"A man had a fig tree, planted in his vineyard, and he went to look for fruit on it, but did not find any." As the story unfolds, it seems that year after year the Man came to check for fruit on this tree and always went away empty. It was a miserable waste-of-space tree, and the patience of the man's Master soon reached its end.

"Cut it down! Why should it use up the soil?"

The rule-keeping, peer-pleasing religion of Jesus' day, with its leafy displays of religiosity, offered precious little by way of real fruit. Its branches were bare of anything you could call brokenhearted faith. They held nothing that tasted like sacrificing love, at least not to God. That's why John the Baptist came crying that God was already holding the ax to the fruitless stump, taking his measure. Judgment was coming and very soon.

But "worthless trees never change" is not the gist of Jesus' story.

In his parable, the Owner of the trees declared, "Cut it down," but there was one man who cried: "Leave it alone for one more year, and I'll dig around it and fertilize it. [I'll do whatever I have to. Let me try.]" In other words, "I can put fruit on that tree."

This is Jesus, the one with his back to a tree, stepping into the space between the unholy trunk and God's gleaming ax. The tree stands for us. The ax is divine judgment drawn all the way back, then crashing down . . . on the Son. While we were sinners—before we had changed in any way—Jesus died to save us. This is love. You can search for it all your life and never find what was in it for Jesus, except to have us with him forever, to hear our puny praise, and to know that we are happy. And when Jesus died, a new thing was released, barely noticeable at first, but neither could it be denied.

A hardened criminal offered a prayer: "Jesus, remember me."

An order-following centurion spoke for himself: "This man was the Son of God."

A timid Pharisee stepped out of the shadows: "May I care for his body?"

A rich man from that empty religion turned to someone to say, "I know of an empty tomb." You can search these words all day and not find what was in it for him.

These are the things that come from faith. The unmistakable flavor of love hangs all about them. This is the sound of people changing. This is the accomplishment of Christ and of his life turned loose in the barren wilderness of the world.

"I can put fruit on that tree."

(Please read Luke 13:6-9.)

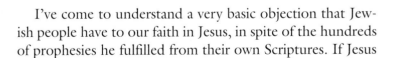

I've come to understand a very basic objection that Jewish people have to our faith in Jesus, in spite of the hundreds of prophesies he fulfilled from their own Scriptures. If Jesus was in any sense the Christ, that is, the Messiah prophesied throughout the Old Testament writings, then why is everything just as it was before? If the idea of Messiah meant anything to the children of Abraham, it meant that the Chosen One would come to change the world. But look around you. Where are the messianic blessings?

Where is the gathering of sons and daughters to one delightful spot? Where is the wine flowing toward them down the hillsides? Where is that ethereal light that shines so that they no longer need the sun or the moon? I ask you, Does the world look changed to you?

This is the same objection that casual observers of Christianity may have on a smaller scale. Some people who "find Jesus" make all kinds of claims about being changed, but are they really? Do the promises of the wife beater who "got religion" reliably stick? Even if there are some differences that can be observed, is it enough to justify such claims as the Bible makes? Are the "children of light" really all that different from the "children of darkness"? Where is the sort of ground-shifting change in people we keep hearing about?

Josh McDowell has a point when he cites the fact that *millions* of people *do* describe a sudden change for the better in the way they experience and carry out their lives, which they report comes to them by faith in Jesus. He issues a challenge for anyone to rebut this point with a single case of atheism changing one life in a comparable way.

Although he's had no takers so far, there's still a better answer to the question of change. It starts with a better question: "Just what *kind* of change did Jesus accomplish on his cross?"

One way the Bible answers is to say, "[Christ] died for all, and therefore all died."[201] When Jesus died for the world, it was as if the entire world had died. The critical thing to grasp is that the change Jesus brought was first of all a complete reversal of status. Think of it like this: if the government in its vast computer network ever got the idea that you died, it would change everything for you. You would be in the category of—have the legal standing of—those who were dead. This new status would have its advantages. The I.R.S. would not come to you for payment of any debt. If you were obliged to serve time in prison for some crime, no one would ever knock on your door. All that would be over. To them, you are dead. And they would not be easily talked out of it.

This is what Christ has done for the entire human world. His punishing death was reckoned by God to be the death of all. Something was spoken about the world in the very throne room of God. It all happened before you and I changed in any way. "I forgive you." You must pause and take it in. As far as God is concerned, it's all over. The condemned world has become the forgiven world. The guilty world has been declared not guilty for Jesus' sake. The world with the sentence of death is now the world completely and utterly redeemed.

This change of status from condemned to forgiven in Christ changes everything. We know who we are. We know whose we are. We have peace. We have hope. We have a future. We have God. Faith in Jesus means that something completely new is written by the Spirit of God at the very bottom of our lives: "I have reconciled you to myself."

And in your soul you know sweetness like red wine rushing down the very hills.

You share a sacred space with everyone who has been gathered into Christ.

All you see and all you see *by* is Christ, your light.

And though everything is the same, *the Messiah changes everything*. Including you. Slowly but surely, and from the inside out, you are being renewed into the very likeness of Christ. When God gives you sorrow over your sin and the gift of trusting in his certain Word, there is something new that begins to stir at that very moment. And this is key: the change in you is not the *cause* of your salvation but its *result*. (This is why the *degree* of change in us is not the cause of either morbid doubt or foolish pride.)

I once heard the entertaining account from a man who spent the first 30 years of his life thinking he was German, then he found out he was really Irish. He described the way this sudden, new fact slowly, strangely worked itself out in his life . . . until the song he sang in the shower was not *"Du, du liegst mir im Herzen,"* but "O Danny Boy." In his words, "Here I thought I was *that* . . . come to find out . . . I'm *this*."

To become a Christian is to wake up to a world of facts. I'm a sinner. This knowledge is unavoidable. I know I'm *that*. However, in Jesus, I've come to find out that I'm *this*—I am a child of the Creator-God, a soul bound for his glory, an object of such love I can scarcely take it in. By God's grace, that truth is ever unfolding, revealing, and working itself out in my life.

I'm not always much to look at it, for my sinful nature is with me still, and no, it doesn't change. My old self is a decrepit, old house of serpentine hallways and dank, dark rooms. It could be explored *ad nauseam* to the fascination of any psychotherapist. I carry the dreadful flesh wherever I go. I am sorry when you have to see it and taste its bitter fruits. Though it is not the real me anymore, I remain ashamed of it and strive for its daily crucifixion. But there is something else that is the real me now, by the power of God, something completely new. There is another place within me and in all who know Christ, another room in this house bathed in a warm, steady light. In my inner being, I am wonderfully alive.

"My Father and I will come and make our home with you," promised Jesus.[202]

And though I still grieve and moan in this same old, same old world, in *that* home and in *that* room the Light never goes out. I am a quiet celebration of the God of my salvation. I know that I will never die. I know what my life is for. That it might somehow result in glory for my Lord is what I want more than anything.

This hidden life—Christ *in* me—is sustained by the power of God's Word and is carried out in the sincerity of daily repentance. I aspire to no higher situation in life than to be as the woman at Jesus' feet whom the Pharisee could not understand for all her tears, her shameless devotion, her desperate clutching. Would that my life, thus altered, cry for explanation just as hers did, and that only this explanation would do:

She loved so much . . . because she was forgiven so much.[203]

Martin Luther groaned: "Lord, I'm tired of making promises to you. You must change me; I cannot change myself." God answers with a pledge: *"I will give you a new heart."*[204] God tells me that his Son lives in me, and I believe him. In this way, a lifetime of bitter struggle to be more, to be better, to be enough has become instead, "Thank you, Jesus." All this goes on beneath the waterline of my seemingly ordinary life. It is the good work of my God that he will certainly finish. *He* will.

Spirit, I'm sorry for the grief I've brought you today.

Jesus, thank you for this peace I've found in you. Only let me know you better.

Father, may I somehow bring honor to you.

This is change. These are the things that any Christian knows about, but that *only* they do. This is the measure of the canyon between the children of light and the children of the dark. All the glory goes to Jesus. *"I can put fruit on that tree."*

You may say that I'm not perfect, and I know the truth of that far better than you.

But God isn't through with me yet. What you can't say is that I am the same as I was.

I'll admit that growing up into Christ doesn't always *feel* like progress. I grieve just a little more now than I did when this journey began. I need Christ in a more basic way. My mind is much quicker to turn back toward him and toward home. When I see him, it will be a sight so beautiful and blessed that I will be brought in a flash, in a twinkling, the rest of the way—finally, fully changed.

I will be like him, and nothing will ever be the same.

"Are Christians really happier?"

Someone has commented that if history is ever to come alive for us, we must resist the perpetual "fast forward." We do not capture the drama in Independence Hall, do not walk in the frozen boots at Valley Forge, do not see the past through the past's eyes, or come anywhere near the courage of those days if we are always mentally peaking ahead—"Well, we all know how *that* turned out." Of course *we* do.

Those who were there did not.

If you have a Christian heart, it could break if you let it visit history's most miserable Saturday and manage to resist the fast forward. You can at least try to make the day come alive, though it refuses. You see, God the Son was dead. Those who had known Jesus awoke into a Christ-less world, too horrible to contemplate. A sword called grief cruelly jutted from Mary's chest. A prison called fear contained the disciples in a lightless, locked room. A millstone called shame almost pulled Peter under. It's a wonder he survived. Judas did not.

Of course, every soul in the upper room could have nursed an inward smile even then. Moments that excluded all happiness might still have held joy. Jesus had made them a promise. He had told them that grief itself would cry tears of sheer delight. He had told them again and again that he would rise. The promise could have been enough for them. They could have merely believed him . . . and have known how it would all turn out.

Shame on them that they didn't.

Thomas did not anticipate his own breathless shout, "My Lord and my God." It caught him by surprise that Sunday morning when the lock of death was broken from the inside.

So very soon Peter would hear the unmistakable Voice call to his boat from the shore. He would pull on his cloak as he would jump into the water (as if he expected to walk across the surface like before) and would sit down to breakfast beside a fire and be served by Jesus . . . like always. In the meantime, his was a needless, gloomy sulk. Like ours.

Behind us are the moments in history that tell us how much we are loved by God because of all that he endured. Ahead of us is the renewal of all things, which began in a first century tomb. And now because Jesus lives, the fast forward is precisely the button we can always push. The ending is carved in Jerusalem stone.

In circumstances that admit no happiness because of all the wishes that didn't turn out, ours is the joy that looks back and ahead, that rises above the merely now . . .

That nothing can touch.

(Please read John chapters 20 and 21.)

Will becoming a Christian finally make you happy?

From hearing the way some of us Christians talk, you might assume that Christianity centers on some sort of guarantee from God for a perfectly pleasant time of it here in this world. Do we have such a promise from God? Will things always work out the way we want them to if we have just the right kind of faith and if (talk about pressure) we can just figure out how to make all the right biblical principles operative in our lives? Nothing could be further from the truth.

The story is told of a man whose horse ran away. His neighbors said: "Oh, what a *bad* thing has happened to you! Terrible. You've lost your horse."

He replied: "You say too much. We don't know what is good or bad. You should only say that my horse ran away."

When the horse came back into the pen, leading a dozen other horses with it, the neighbors gathered to say: "Man, now we know what you mean. What a *good* thing your horse ran away, now you have 12 more. Wonderful!"

The man patiently replied once more: "Once again, you say too much. We don't know what is good or bad. Only say that I now have 13 horses."

One day while the man's son was breaking those horses, he broke his leg. What do you suppose the neighbors had to say? Or what did they say a little later when the country went to war and the son with the broken leg couldn't go? Always they opened their mouths to name one circumstance good and another bad, as if they knew things they could not possibly know, as if they were qualified to answer things no human being can. What *should* happen? What *will* happen a day or even an hour from now? Which events will turn out badly? Which circumstances will work out into happiness?

Always the man replied: "You say too much."

Do you get it?

As for me, it is only with an open Bible in my hand that I can say anything at all for sure. What I say is that our fallen planet is not one designed primarily for our happiness. We respond angrily to trouble as if it is strange and unforeseen, as if life is *supposed* to be easy. However, God does not appear to be concerning himself with our human agenda of making this groaning world a livable place. In my foolishness, *his* agenda—that of gathering people into himself, into the knowledge of his Son—is not one that I properly value. God allows evil that it might serve for greater good. Anyone who believes in the cross—where the ultimate evil wrought the highest conceivable good—ought to know this well enough.

So do not say too much.

Only say that God is immeasurably good and that we can trust him in all things. Only say that his purpose is unfathomably wonderful—to get as many of us home as he can, whatever the cost to himself, whatever the cost to us. This is the greatest good. The rest is trivial.

Only say, "In all things God works for the good of those who love him."[205]

Only ask, "Who shall separate us from the love of Christ?"[206]

Only sigh, "Amen. Come, Lord Jesus."[207]

What then of our normal, human desire for a little bit of happiness while we wait? Forget for the moment that pursuing happiness is a little like trying to fall asleep—some things don't come best by trying to make them come. Happiness is one of those things best thought of as a by-product of character and as a quality of life *that will find us* when we learn to pursue honorable and decent things.

It is important to acknowledge that there are worse problems in my soul than my unhappiness; there are seamy fissures in my character that the Word of God is relentlessly working to reveal. Left to myself, my pursuit of happiness has the disgusting feel of the prodigal son's request. In Jesus' brilliant parable, a young man indirectly says to his father, "I'm tired of waiting for you to die." He wants his father's inheritance . . . *now.* That's me, wanting what God has to give, grasping at his best temporary blessings, thinking I'll find some joy in them *whether I live close to him or not.* And when I lose this or that thing in the world, I despair as if I have lost it all. Shame on me.

While I was running from him, chasing happiness, he was running toward me, sprinting toward the pain it would cost to have me back. We call it our theology of the cross. This refers to the fact that God has always done his best things in this world through weakness, pain, and apparent defeat. For think of what God accomplished through nails and a spear and willing flesh. When you're unhappy, go ahead and find some solitude where you can beat on God's chest a while and ask all your tear-streaked questions. Just don't forget to contemplate his answer, the dying God embracing the dying cosmos. Just be sure that when you're sad, so sad, you don't say *too much.*

Only say, "God so loved the world . . ."

Only say, God has "made his light shine in our hearts to give us the light of the knowledge of the glory of God in the face of Christ."[208] The greatest gift is God's gracious presence itself: to walk out into the sun and let the Spirit open up the words and to know them. "There is now no condemnation for those who are in Christ."[209] This time it is God who seems to say far, far too much. But there it is. We are ushered into the truest desire for the highest delight as we sigh with the apostles, "I want to know Christ."[210]

And call it devil-inspired blindness to prefer any other blasted thing in this world to the treasure of simply knowing him, knowing we are forgiven, and knowing that our story winds up in him. We are frustrated and sad, angry and in despair for all the things we desire more than we desire him. For to me, to live is . . . what? stable family? meaningful career? nice friends? No. "For to me, to live *is Christ.*"

"And to die is gain."[211] That is to say, it is sheer foolishness to live, even for a moment, as if this life is anything but a prelude to another that is better by far.

Ask the apostles if Christians are happy, and I expect they would shrug their shoulders, not knowing quite what you mean or what the question has to do with anything. It's not about happiness for them. It's about joy, that unique Christian joy. I submit that the subjective experience of millions of believers does count for further confirmation of Christianity, anchored as it is to historic fact and objective reality. You may dismiss it as mere psychology, as if all the truth about such things as being in love or finding God is captured by the scientific point of view, by those who coolly analyze such experiences from the outside. It is just as easy to say that those who have seen this joy, this Jesus, from the inside know something those who haven't seen it cannot comprehend.

It is for the sake of joy that the apostles first followed the least manipulative call in history: "If anyone would come after me, he must deny himself and take up his cross and follow me."[212] And they called it worthwhile. After all, while we wait to see the face of Christ, that great glistening light at the end of our mortal tunnel . . . they already have.

The best man, called the *Soshben,* stands watch outside the bridal chamber. When the groom arrives, their eyes meet. "I knew you'd come," whispers the best man, and he relishes the groom's answer: "There's no one else I would have trusted for this."

And in rabbinic law, when the groom and bride have been brought together, only one thing remains for the Soshben. He is to go away rejoicing.

"That joy is mine," said John the Baptist.

This was the picture that formed in his mind when folks thought he should be sad or even angry that his whirlwind career as prophet was over. All his circumstances were moving from the unpleasant toward the gruesome and tragic. He was going away.

But he had introduced the Bridegroom, Christ, to Israel, his bride.

He had known Jesus, and he had made Jesus known. "That joy is mine."[213]

"Religion

only puts

barriers

between

people"

Do you remember the Tower of Babel? I refer to the biblical account of the outrageous pride of humanity and to the great separation and dispersion of people that resulted. When men were attempting to erect a tower to heaven as a colossal monument to themselves, God intervened and "confused the language of the whole world."[214]

In this way, he humbled the people, frustrated their arrogant plans, and fractured the community united against him. In reality, people had stopped making sense to one another long before this. The human clay pot had long before been shattered. If the language barrier hadn't separated the people at Babel, eventually, inevitably something else would have. Did I mention how proud they were?

Now I invite your consideration of the great mirror-image story in the New Testament, the great regathering of nations that occurred at Pentecost, the humbling and hopeful undoing of Babel.

Jerusalem. Into an upper room filled with prayer like incense and to the faithful disciples who were waiting for the Spirit of the resurrected Jesus came the sound of wind and the flicker of flames. Unschooled Galileans suddenly had the power to speak the unstudied tongues of Parthians, Medes, Elamites . . . and of anyone else who happened to be standing nearby. The wonder of how the disciples overcame the age-old language barrier recedes to the wonder of what they actually said. Peter declared that the people of Jerusalem had crucified God's Son—a horrid act, unspeakably wrong—but the very thing that was their salvation. God's Son was alive.

And though they were Parthians, Medes, and Elamites, they understood Peter. This day was the work of the Holy Spirit, who is always at work, always pointing, always revealing, always drawing us all toward Jesus.

When the people together had their hearts broken and were together made afraid for all they had done, they were together shown mercy. In this sorrow and this peace, they found the only path back to God and, as it turns out, the only path back to one another. They became a fellowship of grace such as the world had never seen, speaking the common language of love. They were baptized for the forgiveness of their sins—Parthians, Medes, Elamites, and all the rest of the three thousand.

They were washed into the name of Jesus Christ.

The Barrier Breaker.

(Please read Acts chapter 2.)

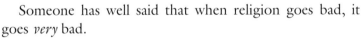

Someone has well said that when religion goes bad, it goes *very* bad.

It's an ugly thing when the Muslim hates the Hindu, when the Jew hates the Christian, when the Christian hates *anyone.* So you ask, "What good is religion if it only knows how to exclude, if it only erects barriers between people, sectioning them off into synagogues, mosques, and churches, and then again into cliques, sects, and denominations?" One more time I pause to acknowledge the true instinct behind a common objection to Christianity. No, this is not the way it's supposed to be. All people should be one family. That they are not is tragic. All the labels, all the talk about who's really right, all the scowling over the fences of our own design—something has gone terribly wrong in this humanity carved up into petty, competing pieces. But what?

I would suggest that it's a little naïve to blame the problems of the world on the Christian faith. It is Jesus, only Jesus, who gave the world the command, "Love your enemies,"[215] not to mention the compelling reason to actually *want* to. No other ethic has ever reached so high or so far. The notion is absurd that this would be a better place if the influence of Christ were somehow removed.

It is true enough that the world is full of bickering false religions as well as corrupted, Christ-less versions of Christianity. But even they do not have a monopoly on the barrier-building business. Only notice that there are plenty of places in the world where religion is not the excuse for hostility between people but political ideology is instead. And if not ideology, then gender, then race. And where people don't hiss and spit across racial lines, they do over economic ones. Fiercely. You may drill it into children in the classroom, "All gods are alike, and you are all the same," but it won't keep them from being cruel on the playground. Go ahead, and "imagine no religion" right along with John Lennon. People will still find a reason to hate.

Once again I say that it is not religion that deserves the indictment. You have to look a little deeper. It's humanity itself. Something is really wrong with us, in fact, something only Christianity adequately names, properly describes, or seriously confronts. Only Christianity truly deals with the part of me that hates and hides and harbors all kinds of foolish things . . . the part of me that is a horror to me, that I rise up to condemn, that I would crucify again and again.

While every other attempt to name that part of me is hacking about the leaves, it's the ancient word *sin* that strikes at the root and succinctly describes the human dilemma. Whether we're talking about pride or self-centeredness, anger or hatred, lust or the shame that comes as a result, it is the very nature of sin to cause separations. Sin kills relationships, walling us each off in our little worlds of private, fearful concerns. It always has. It always will. We hunger and ache and long to be true kindreds with someone, anyone, and may even seem to find that . . . for a time. But sin runs its course, and we end up alone. Alone and angry, or alone and ashamed, or alone and afraid . . . but always alone. The way back is blocked by our own egos, like dressers shoved against a door. Call to mind especially that peculiar loneliness of the child who would rather miss the party than say that he is sorry.

The self-inflicted wound and the empty horizontal space that opens up around every human soul is merely a dim reflection of the very worst that sin does. For that, think vertically: "Your iniquities have separated you from your God."[216]

It is only holy and right that God should turn his face and remove his presence from this fractured humanity that bears no resemblance to him. And if we somehow don't feel his absence, it is only an indication of how far gone we are.

Modern psychology treats people as merely wounded and views the *self* as something like a damaged *thing* that requires the ingenuity of professionals if it is to be figured out and fixed. But that's not it at all. We are separated souls. We are withering spirits, having long been cut off from him who is Life and Love and everything Good. We will never come alive unless we somehow find connection with God. And only in being brought back to God can we ever really be given back to one another.

Although falsely practiced religion ultimately separates, as does everything else merely human, only Christianity can work the other way. For there is a moment that only Christianity contains. When God himself could no longer bear the separation, his Son "died for the ungodly."[217] Here is the one fact in this whole predictable, nothing-new-under-the-sun world that manages to be a surprise again and again and again: God gave us Christ when we were "hostile to God,"[218] when we were "powerless,"[219] when we were "still sinners."[220] And when it happened, deep within the Jewish temple in Jerusalem, a thick, non-permeable veil that covered the entrance to the Most Holy Place just tore in two. The way was opened to the very presence of God, leaving nothing standing between him and us anymore. Can you imagine? "What shall I give you? I give you myself." The sound of that tearing and that giving is still heard.

In Christ, God had taken it upon himself to teach brotherly love, and Christ's death was the breathtaking start to our education. God wins our hearts with his love. And when we find that God has been merciful to us, for Jesus' sake, we are made ready to be merciful. We, forgiven, are newly empowered to forgive. We learn that what God has done for us, we owe to our human sisters and brothers, even our enemies. Jesus is the only one compelling me to move toward them in order to love them. He is the only good reason. He is the only hope for oneness between me and people who are different from me in every way except in knowing Jesus. I hear the Name exulted in a foreign tongue. The talk is all *Jesu* or *Hesoos* or *Iasou*. And I know just what they mean.

I've had people in my congregation and in my classroom from Sweden and Antigua, from India and Japan, from corporate headquarters and from the inner city of Milwaukee, Wisconsin. As I write I've just returned from a month in Cameroon, West Africa, and I found the same undoing of Babel in the open-air markets of Kumba-town.

The only location in the world where we can ever hope to meet is in Christ.

When we are *in Christ*, this simple faith is the DNA, the stuff at the center that says we belong to one another just as the stunningly diverse members of a body perfectly fit together. In the deepest place—deeper than color, richer than culture, transcending mere tolerance, more personal than any mere human affinity—*we are the same in Jesus.* Those who know Jesus have *fellowship* with God and so also *fellowship* with one another—this biblical word names your desire for oneness. It is a place that, in spite of our sin, we can always get back to. It is found in the perpetual repenting and in the constant confessing—*the together saying*—"I believe in Jesus Christ, his only Son, our Lord. . . ." And no, it's not wrong to go looking for a kindred soul, to rejoice at having found one, and to know that you are not alone.

Now, to be honest, there are times when Christian churches must draw regretful but appropriate lines between people. To understand why, only remember that the primary issue of this book is concerned with the truth or falsehood of Christ crucified and Christ raised from the dead. If he is true, then please notice how every word spoken in support of his truth (no matter who had to hear that they were wrong), every gap pointed out between those who are for and those who are against him (no matter whose feelings were hurt), and every single word of rebuke spoken to a secure sinner (though it didn't seem like love at the time) . . . *is vindicated.*

These are the right, the honest, the compassionate things to do if Jesus is true. If he is alive, just as Peter and the Spirit declared, all arguments to the contrary vanish like smoke.

If only the space between us would as well.

Connection. I am not condemned to isolation in this skin of mine, behind these two eyes. In the harmony of the hymns while you and I worship . . . in the feel of your shoulder and in the scent that lingers about you as we say that we believe "in the communion of saints, the forgiveness of sins" . . . in, with, and under the bread and the wine . . . I—we—taste the stuff of heaven.

CONCLUSION

"What is God up to in the world?"

If God is not doing the sorts of things we humans think he should be doing—rumors of wars still rustle in all the leaves and death still rattles around in the weeds—well, then, what is he doing? What is he up to? Where *can* we find him?

The Lord is in his temple.

One way to trace God's presence and his activity on earth is to follow that symbol, the temple, from the earliest days of salvation history to the present time.[221] A temple is, simply, the place where God lives.

In Old Testament times, God's temple was an awesome—sometimes holy-smoke-filled—edifice on Mount Zion in Jerusalem. There was met the terrible holiness of God, the fierce justice the people could not stand. The perfect cube-shaped room in the center, the Most Holy Place, where God's special presence dwelled, was not only holy. It was dangerous. Once each year the high priest entered the Most Holy Place with bells hanging from the hems of his garments. That way the people could hear whether he was still moving around inside. If he wasn't, they could pull him out by the rope he had tied around his waist. The message that arrived with the temple—woven into the fabric, reflecting off the gold, drifting with the smoke—was both overpowering and necessary. "There is a God, and you're not him. Take him seriously. Perceive the gap between holiness and iniquity. If the truth is in you, tremble at the thought of him."

But that wasn't the only message. There was always one thing more: "Don't be afraid. You need God to have mercy on you . . . and he will." The people were only to think of the lambs and then know that God himself would find a way.

History records that when Jerusalem fell its great fall, the Babylonian soldiers crept terrified into that temple, jabbing spears in the air at the invisible God of the Hebrews, the one the whole world trembled at. But if he was there anymore, he didn't let on. Because of the disgraceful forgetting by his own people, the Israelites, you might say that God moved.

Fast forward. You've been to Jerusalem. Now go to Bethlehem. Love and Truth were embodied in a helpless infant, then an obedient boy, then a humble and gentle man. Here "the fullness of the Deity live[d],"[222] so he called his body, simply, this temple. In this entire secular world, the place to go to find Divinity and to fall in worship . . . was at the feet of Christ. That's where Mary sat listening to Jesus talk, just talk. It was her "one necessary thing." She crumpled into his shadow when her brother died, and Jesus' spirit crumpled beside her. She always ran for sanctuary to the warm and touchable Jesus.

"Destroy this temple," Jesus once said, "And in three days I will raise it up again." In Christ, God would put himself at our mercy, knowing we had none. "Destroy this temple. Do your worst—pound on its walls, rip its fabric off in layers, hammer and scar and deface it and lay it to the ground—and I will raise it up again." At the crucifixion of Christ, a soldier approached, jabbing his spear into God's holy sanctuary. But Jesus' spirit had gone.

On the third day following the horrendous judicial murder of Jesus, he is found alive and Mary is found where we always find her, grasping his feet. On that early Sunday morning when the world woke up redeemed, Mary was holding on for dear life, all her enemies dead, even death itself. In Christ's death, God spoke gentle words with a gathering power: "I have forgiven you."

Today, where in this whole world are we to find God's temple? "Don't you know that *you* yourselves are God's temple and that God's Spirit *lives in you?*"[223] puzzled the apostle. God is on the move . . . again. Through the Holy Spirit, the worldwide congregation of believers in Jesus is now the place where Divinity lives. This is where God is found. He is building in this world a sanctuary, a place for himself, constructed from the "living stones"[224] of people who know his Son and believe.

The Christian church is what God is up to in the world.

We gather into Christ by faith, warming our hands over an open Bible, satiating ourselves with bread that is body, quenching ourselves with wine that is blood, washing our faces in cool, baptismal water. He will come for us soon, so we wait in him, filling his place with prayers like incense. Compared to messages given through shaking mountains and thundering prophets of Old Testament times, the message from his Spirit is the most quiet and quenchable of all . . . and the most intimate. Christ speaks with a still, small voice. And he is closer to you than he was to Mary as he sat right beside her.

"I am *in* you now, just as you are in me. Together we'll be. Forever."

(Please read the Bible.)

What is God up to in this world?

The scriptural answer centers on the Christian church, which may come as a bit of a shock. At first glance you see all the marks of a human institution—buildings and bulletins, budgets and bottom lines. I've dealt honestly with the blemishes of the visible church in several chapters of my two books. Yet if all you see is another flawed human institution, I ask you to look again. This time listen for a heartbeat and check for a pulse. Witness the living organism that transcends mere institution. Observe the Christian church. It has not come so far on the winds of a lie; it has not dared to exist for the sake of a myth. Lifeless things sink or else float along with the force of the river. It has taken the living body of Christ to swim upstream against every current of human history.

I make a critical distinction between human institutions and the body of believers in Jesus. Consider institutions such as Yale and Harvard universities, which were originally founded as "divinity schools" devoted to the reverent study of Jesus by the Word of God. Then consider nominal Christian churches where Christ crucified is no longer preached. When the spiritual life dies and the divine light goes out, the buildings don't come crashing down. Instead, notice how easily the institutions continue along. Human structures can always perpetuate themselves all on their own steam, driven by the "basic principles of this world,"[225] those mundane ambitions and self-flatteries that also drive mere human beings.

Here lies the difference. The living body of Christ and all those bonded to him in the sincerity of faith cannot go one day, *not one day,* if God does not sustain them by his power. This is what he is up to in the world. His community, alive with faith in Jesus and the love that comes from him, would die instantly if it were not for the fact that Christ "feeds and cares for" his body,[226] literally, he keeps it warm.

The Word of God tells us again and again, over and over, what we could otherwise never believe—the one thing that is essential and defining to the Christian life—that we sinners are reconciled to God through the gift of his Son. His mercy is "new every morning"[227] simply because it has to be, or else we die. As the Word keeps faith alive within us . . .

Christ is feeding his body.

I remember the overwhelming grace I experienced in my 12 years in the pastoral ministry—hands grasping other hands as forgiveness was proclaimed, eyes glistening as the bread was taken, contagious spreading smiles when one of us celebrated, and the tight circling of Christians when one of us grieved. And I see what God is up to.

Christ is keeping his body warm.

God did not give his church a good, strong push at Pentecost and leave us to carry the movement ourselves. Every newborn baby comes into the world spiritually dead, cut adrift from God as sinful human nature continues to perpetuate itself. Flesh gives birth to flesh gives birth to flesh. Each soul to be added to Christ requires a fresh work and a new miracle. With the water on tiny foreheads and the words, " _(Your name here)_ , I baptize you in the name of the Father and of the Son and of the Holy Spirit," God always shows up in his church with grace in fresh supply, "cleansing her by the washing with water through the word."[228]

We know God is active in the world because the Christian church, the body of true believers, exists. It is an unworldly kind of power that "made us alive with Christ even when we were dead,"[229] and that allows us to continue to be what we are. Who are we? We are the blessed ones, the ones who "grasp how wide and long and high and deep is the love of Christ,"[230] the ones who walk the path that runs past the skull-shaped hill, who look up at Jesus and know just what we are seeing. We know what it cost him to be our God and to love us as he does. We know where we would be without him.

I know you have your questions. The great irony in the skeptic's challenges is how many of these challenges God saw fit to write into his own Book.

How can we believe God even notices us on this dirty tennis ball called earth? "What is man that [God is] mindful of him?"[231]

Where is this God of power and love?

"How long, O LORD? Will you forget me forever?"[232]

I honor the questions, even as God did. These struggles of ours are the dreadful tip of the iceberg of the world's estrangement from God. "Do not be surprised at the painful trial you are suffering, as though something strange were happening to you."[233] In a word? *Hard.* God knows life is hard. Worth it, to be sure. But hard.

But I notice also that such Old Testament questions as those loudly wailed by the little prophets all but disappear in the New. They seem just to fade from the minds of those who saw Christ alive after they saw him die. Let that stand as the theme of everything I'm writing to you. If you can get down to what your heart is really asking in all your questions, the answer is always Jesus. See him alive.

The seeming withdrawal of God from a darkening world—how many people are crying as you sit and read—is no reason for us to wring our hands. Things are never what they seem. God is here. God is with us. In a wicked and depraved generation, we find our opportunity to be different, to be set apart, to be a city on a hill, *to be his church.* So let the story go out. That's all I'm trying to say. Tell his story.

For you *"shine like stars . . . as you hold out the word of life."*[234]

Like stars.

Between the close of New Testament revelation in the first century to the very close of time, we live in what may be called the Church Age. And no, it hasn't been easy.

Imagine the scene if you can stand it. Picture the Christian mommies and daddies and children herded out of the dark where they were held into the dusty circle, squinting and shielding their eyes from the sunshine they hadn't seen in days. The first thing that assaults them is the noise, a huge human noise, with animal sounds mixed in. As their eyes adjust, they see people looking on, thousands of people. And lions.

Rome.

They huddle together, terrified and full of courage. Softly at first someone begins the "Te Deum," the dry and dusty words, so you say, of the ancient liturgy, the "You-O-God."

We praise you, O God, we acclaim you as Lord; all creation worships you, Father everlasting. . . . heaven and earth are full of your glory.

The crowd grows impatient. Let it start already. A father pushes a little girl's head to his chest . . . "Close your eyes, sweetie. I'm here. Sing with me, darling, you know the words."

The glorious company of apostles praise you. The noble fellowship of prophets praise you. The white-robed army of martyrs praise you.

The man pulls his wife even closer and turns her face up. His eyes say, "Look only at me," and he manages a hint of a smile, for her . . . for him. And he chants louder now:

Throughout the world the holy Church acclaims you: Father of majesty unbounded, your glorious, true, and only Son, and the Holy Spirit, advocate and guide.

Friends are cut down . . . but not ashamed. Torn apart . . . but the center holds. Jesus, forgive me everything . . . everything . . . and into your hands I give . . . my spirit.

When you became man to set us free, you humbled yourself to be born of a virgin. You overcame the sting of death and opened the kingdom of heaven to all believers. Come then, Lord, and help your people, bought with the price of your own blood.

Not long now . . . my last breath . . . to you, O God. Ah, *Te Deum.*

And bring us with your saints to glory everlasting.

Amen and amen.

ENDNOTES

[1] 1 Corinthians 1:25
[2] Matthew 16:18
[3] Luke 10:21
[4] John 6:63
[5] Jeremiah 29:11
[6] Jeremiah 29:13,14
[7] Psalm 13:6
[8] Matthew 14:27
[9] Colossians 3:4
[10] John 3:16
[11] Matthew 3:17 (KJV)
[12] See Philippians 2:8.
[13] Matthew 4:3,4
[14] Hebrews 1:2
[15] Francis Thompson, *The Hound of Heaven.*
[16] 1 Timothy 2:5
[17] 1 John 5:20
[18] 1 Corinthians 2:8
[19] Acts 20:28
[20] Romans 9:25 (KJV)
[21] Adapted from G. K. Chesterton.
[22] Matthew 8:11
[23] Acts 4:12
[24] Hebrews 10:20,22
[25] 1 Peter 3:15
[26] John 14:6
[27] Adapted from G. K. Chesterton.
[28] G. K. Chesterton, *Orthodoxy* (Wheaton, IL: Harold Shaw Publishers, 1994), p. 107.

[29]Jeremiah 31:3

[30]2 Peter 1:21

[31]Genesis 15:6

[32]Psalm 16:9,10

[33]Job 19:25-27

[34]John 5:39

[35]John W. Montgomery, *History and Christianity* (Downers Grove, IL: InterVarsity Press, 1971).

[36]Matthew 24:35

[37]Isaiah 40:8

[38]John 10:27

[39]John 3:19

[40]Psalm 46:10

[41]1 Timothy 1:15

[42]1 John 1:1

[43]A. N. Sherwin-White, *Roman Society and Roman Law in the New Testament* (Grand Rapids: Baker Book House, 1978).

[44]Paul E. Little, *Know Why You Believe* (Colorado Springs: Cook Communications, 1999), p. 77.

[45]Paul E. Little, *Know Why You Believe,* p. 88.

[46]2 Peter 1:16

[47]Luke 18:31

[48]Matthew 24:14

[49]Jeremiah 31:3

[50]Matthew 5:45

[51]Genesis 1:3

[52]Hebrews 11:3

[53]Steve Turner, *Up to Date* (London: Hodder & Stoughton, 1985). Quoted in Ravi Zecharias, *Can Man Live without God* (Dallas: Word Publishing, 1994), p. 44.

[54]Job 38:3,4

[55]Luke 12:27

[56]Lamentations 3:23

[57]Adapted from G. K. Chesterton.

[58]Adapted from G. K. Chesterton.

[59]1 Corinthians 6:19,20

[60]Isaiah 49:15

[61]Jeremiah 31:3

[62]Jeremiah 2:13

[63]1 Corinthians 1:18,20

[64]Revelation 1:7

[65]Job 42:3

[66]1 Timothy 6:16

[67]Isaiah 55:9

[68]2 Corinthians 10:5

[69]John 3:16

[70]Psalm 131:1,2

[71]Matthew 7:5

[72]1 Corinthians 6:9,10

[73]1 Corinthians 6:11

[74]Isaiah 64:6

[75]Hebrews 5:7

[76]Hebrews 2:18

[77]Matthew 19:26

[78]Romans 6:1

[79]Romans 6:2

[80]Acts 14:22

[81]Romans 9:15

[82]Acts 17:28

[83]Luke 14:33

[84]Matthew 11:28

[85]2 Corinthians 6:1,2

[86]Luke 12:20

[87]Matthew 13:44

[88]Hebrews 9:27

[89]Micah 5:2

[90]Isaiah 7:14

[91]Matthew 27:46

[92]Psalm 103:12

[93]John 1:51

[94]Paul E. Little, *Know Why You Believe*, p. 153.

[95]2 Timothy 3:2

[96]2 Corinthians 4:4

[97]John 8:44

[98]John 12:31,32

[99]Nahum 1:8

[100]Nahum 2:13

[101]Isaiah 43:1

[102]C. S. Lewis, *Weight of Glory* (San Francisco: Harper San Francisco, 1941), p. 26.

[103]John 3:17

[104]John 12:31

[105]1 John 5:1

[106]Psalm 73:25

[107]*Christian Worship: A Lutheran Hymnal* (Milwaukee: Northwestern Publishing House, 1993), 415:3.

[108]Acts 1:14

[109]John 14:6

[110]John 14:6

[111]Ephesians 4:15

[112]2 Thessalonians 2:11

[113]Psalm 103:10

[114]Galatians 3:1

[115]Romans 8:18

[116]Hebrews 12:9

[117]Romans 8:28

[118]Isaiah 53:3

[119]Dylan Thomas, *Do Not Go Gentle into That Good Night.*

[120]Ecclesiastes 3:11

[121]Adapted from C. S. Lewis.

[122]Romans 6:23

[123]Isaiah 25:7,8

[124]Romans 11:16

[125]John 14:19

[126]John 11:25

[127]John 8:34

[128]John 8:36

[129]Galatians 3:13

[130]Philippians 3:9

[131]John 14:19

[132]Philippians 3:10

[133]Martin Luther, *What Luther Says: An Anthology,* compiled by Ewald M. Plass, Vol. 3 (St. Louis: Concordia Publishing House, 1959), p. 1345.

[134]Dorothy L. Sayers, *Are Women Human?* (Downers Grove, IL: Inter-Varsity Press, 1971), p. 47.

[135]Galatians 3:28

[136]Deuteronomy 33:29

[137]1 Corinthians 11:3

[138]Proverbs 31:10

[139]Aldous Huxley, *Ends and Means* (London: Chatto & Windus, 1946), p. 273.

[140]Quoted in Ravi Zecharias, *Can Man Live without God,* p. 105.

[141]Matthew 25:40

[142]Ecclesiastes 1:14

[143]Os Guinness, *Long Journey Home: A Guide to Your Search for the Meaning of Life* (New York: Random House, 2001), p. 6.

[144]Psalm 98:7,8

[145]Dietrich Bonhoeffer, *Letters and Papers from Prison* (New York: Simon & Schuster, 1953), p. 221.

[146]Philemon 6

[147]John 4:35

[148]Colossians 4:3

[149]Ephesians 5:1

[150]Ephesians 4:15

[151]Revelation 22:17

[152]Psalm 145:15,16 (KJV)

[153]Psalm 115:2

[154]Psalm 118:6

[155]Psalm 118:29

[156]Psalm 145:16

[157]Lamentations 3:22,23

[158]Harold L. Senkbeil, *Sanctification: Christ in Action* (Milwaukee: Northwestern Publishing House, 1989), p. 179.

[159]Psalm 51:10,11

[160]Matthew 26:12

[161]1 Timothy 3:3 (KJV). The NIV translates simply "money."

[162]Matthew 6:21

[163]1 Timothy 6:17

[164]Luke 12:15

[165]1 Timothy 6:10

[166]1 Peter 1:7

[167]1 Timothy 6:19

[168]1 John 4:19

[169]John 1:29

[170]Galatians 6:7,8

[171]1 John 3:4

[172]Jeremiah 4:23

[173]John 1:29

[174]Dietrich Bonhoeffer, *Letters and Papers from Prison*, p. 221.

[175]1 John 3:20

[176]Isaiah 54:7

[177]Luke 22:19

[178]Romans 6:3

[179]Lamentations 3:23

[180]Matthew 18:20

[181]John 13:27

[182]Paul E. Little, *Know Why You Believe*, p. 165.

[183]Romans 7:18

[184]Matthew 15:19

[185]1 John 4:7,8

[186]1 Corinthians 2:9

[187]Mark 10:32

[188]Isaiah 50:7

[189]Matthew 16:15

[190]C. S. Lewis, *Mere Christianity* (New York: MacMillan, 1952), p. 56.

[191]Matthew 26:64

[192]John 8:46

[193]Lee Strobel, *The Case for Christ* (Grand Rapids: Zondervan Publishing House, 1998), p. 254.

[194]Philip Schaff, *The Person of Christ* (New York: American Tract Society, 1913). Quoted in Josh McDowell, *The New Evidence that Demands a Verdict* (Nashville: Thomas Nelson Publishers, 1999), p. 15.

[195]1 Corinthians 15:3

[196]Lee Strobel, *The Case for Christ*, p. 260.

197 Philip Schaff, *History of the Christian Church,* Vol. 1 (Grand Rapids: William B. Eerdmans Publishing Company, 1962), p. 109, emphasis added.

198 2 Corinthians 5:19

199 Acts 3:19

200 John 14:1

201 2 Corinthians 5:14

202 John 14:23

203 Luke 7:47

204 Ezekiel 36:26

205 Romans 8:28

206 Romans 8:35

207 Revelation 22:20

208 2 Corinthians 4:6

209 Romans 8:1

210 Philippians 3:10

211 Philippians 1:21

212 Matthew 16:24

213 John 3:29

214 Genesis 11:9

215 Matthew 5:44

216 Isaiah 59:2

217 Romans 5:6

218 Romans 8:7

219 Romans 5:6

220 Romans 5:8

221 Indebted to Philip Yancey for this line of thinking about the word *temple. Disappointment with God* (New York: Harper Collins Publishers, 1988).

222 Colossians 2:9

223 1 Corinthians 3:16

224 1 Peter 2:5

225 Colossians 2:8

226 Ephesians 5:29

227 Lamentations 3:23

228 Ephesians 5:26

229 Ephesians 2:5

[230]Ephesians 3:18
[231]Psalm 8:4
[232]Psalm 13:1
[233]1 Peter 4:12
[234]Philippians 2:15,16